101 TOP TIPS FOR PROPERTY INVESTMENT SUCCESS

by Nick Fox

ISBN: 978-0-9935074-9-6

First published in England in 2016 by Fox Print Partners
Edited by Sarah Walker

101 TOP TIPS FOR PROPERTY INVESTMENT SUCCESS

by Nick Fox

published by Fox Print Partners

Contents

FINDING AND BUYING A PROPERTY

RENOVATION, REFURBISHMENT & GETTING READY TO RENT

LETTING & MANAGING

ONWARDS & UPWARDS

For my family, friends and business partners.
You all inspire me daily. Thank you.
Nick

About the author

A prolific and highly successful investor, Nick Fox has been involved with property since his early childhood. Today, his investment portfolio includes more than 200 buy to let properties – both shared accommodation and single household lets – and he has interests in a number of development projects.

As is the case with so many successful businesspeople, Nick started young. When he was eight, he bought up all the penny sweets from the Scout Camp tuck shop and sold them on to his friends for 2p! His delight at doubling his money on his first business venture signposted an entrepreneurial attitude and launched an enthusiasm for making money on his own terms that has never left him.

His introduction to the property market came not long afterwards, when the caravan that he lived in with his mother burned down. She used the insurance money to buy a wreck of a house, which she did up and sold for a profit, repeating the process until they had a nice home. When he wasn't in school, Nick helped his mother out and began to understand not only what could be achieved by hard work, but also the potential of property as a money-making vehicle. He just needed a bit of capital to get him started.

In 1988, at the age of 19, Nick landed a job with a company that imported computer software from America and sold it into retailers in the UK. It didn't take long for Nick to see the technology boom that was starting and he quickly realised he could do the same thing himself.

Operating out of his bedroom, Nick took out as many credit cards as he could and bought software stock from all over the world. He started off selling into small retailers, then, when the market for personal computers really took off, he moved into proper premises and grew the company until it became the UK's leading budget software company, selling over a million units every month into Dixons, Woolworths and WHSmith.

But by 2002 business had peaked. Technology had gone mainstream and was even available in supermarkets, and things quickly declined for Nick.

2005 was the 'light bulb' moment, when he realised that the income from his various businesses might have paid for his lifestyle, but it was his home that had built equity and given him a lump-sum return. He knew that the quickest and only way he could replace his financial losses was to buy more properties.

By the end of 2005, Nick had five properties, all rented to friends, generating an income and building equity. He started buying larger homes, which he rented as single units to families, and by the end of the following year, Nick had 20 properties and a significant buy to let business.

In 2007, he went into a buying frenzy. Within 12 months, he'd added another 90 properties to his portfolio. Then, as the credit crunch hit and many of his mortgages moved off initial low fixed rates and onto variables, Nick started to look at how he could increase his profits and turned one of his existing family home lets into an HMO. That was light bulb moment number two.

He began to partner with other investors and subsequently doubled the size of his portfolio to more than 200 properties, around 100 of them HMOs. That portfolio is currently managed through the Milton Keynes letting agency he set up in 2010 and achieves 98% occupancy.

"Everyone thinks I must be constantly working to keep so many plates spinning but, really, I just employ great managers and develop effective systems."

Nick's HMO investment strategy is now highly regarded within the industry and he is regularly asked to speak at property investment events. His expertise is called on by new clients and fellow professional investors alike and his reputation has enabled him to establish a significant mentoring business.

Over the past few years, Nick has also acquired business interests outside property: a photography company that he's looking to franchise and investment in a local pre-school that serves 80 children and has been rated 'outstanding' by OFSTED.

Nick loves football, tennis, golf and boating and has climbed Mount Snowdon with his partner, Samantha. He is committed to supporting local charitable causes and is also a Patron of Peace One Day. He and Samantha live just outside St Albans with their five children.

The distance between your dreams and reality is called 'Action'

Author's disclaimer

I am not qualified to give financial or legal advice. All related recommendations made in this book should only be considered in consultation with suitably qualified and accredited professionals. Persons giving financial advice MUST be properly qualified and regulated by the Financial Services Authority (FSA) and anyone giving you legal advice should be suitably qualified and regulated by The Law Society and the Solicitors Regulation Authority (SRA) (or the Council of Licensed Conveyancers (CLC)).

Also by Nick Fox:

HMO Property Success

The Secrets of Buy to Let Success

Property Investment Success

Complete Property Investment Success

HMO Property Renovation & Refurbishment Success

Available in paperback from nickfox.co.uk & Amazon.co.uk
Audiobook available from Amazon.co.uk and Audible.co.uk
Kindle and iBook formats also available

PREPARING YOURSELF AND YOUR BUSINESS

Tip 1

Don't try to do it alone

Before you take any financial or physical step, you must understand that to be successful in property investment you need help. And that help should come from a variety of places: your family, professional advisors, skilled contractors and other investors.

Your family and friends

The whole buy to let process is demanding and can be stressful, and it will be a whole lot easier if you have the support of those closest to you. Not only that, but you'll also need their understanding, as – certainly for the first few years – you're not going to have as much time to spend with them as you do now and they'll need to bear with you and appreciate that you're putting in these long hours now to build a secure future.

Professional advisors

The legal, financial and property industry-specific knowledge and expertise required to acquire, build and run a property portfolio is immense. So engage and make good use of people who are trained, qualified and have the experience to be able to advise and assist you properly, because if you try to scrabble by with the bare minimum, you're likely to run into serious problems.

Contractors & tradespeople

I've met so many investors who have tried to save money by doing what they perceive as the simpler jobs themselves. You may be able to make a reasonable enough job of painting, tiling and fitting units yourself, but I don't think you *should*. Using professional tradespeople and skilled contractors not only means you'll get a professional finish, but they'll also know how to deal with any problems that come up, get the whole job done as quickly as possible and – very importantly - you'll also have a guarantee for the work.

Other investors

You can learn so much from people who've been there and done it before, so take advantage of their experience. Most people are happy to share their knowledge, so network with investors in your area and build reciprocal relationships.

Get some help from:

*   Landlords.org.uk – search for associations in your area
*   Checkatrade.com – for reputable tradespeople

....

"In the end, all business operations can be reduced to three words: people, product and profits. Unless you've got a good team, you can't do much with the other two."

Lee Iacocca

Tip 2

Be clear about why you're doing this

If you don't know what you're trying to achieve, how can you achieve it? Far too many people invest in property 'because it's always a good investment', and that's simply not true. It depends what you want from it.

Do you want to amass some capital as soon as possible? Do you want to build a pension pot? Do you want income now or in retirement? Is it something to leave to your children? How much do you need and when do you need it by? Do you want a project and, if so, part time or full time?

Your answers will affect what you buy - the type of property and location – and how you let it. Property investment is a diverse sector of the market and the financial rewards vary greatly. And if you don't make the right move, it could end up being more of a millstone round your neck than the wealth generator you intended.

Ultimately, you should be doing this because you've had a good look around at other money-making vehicles, researched what investing in property involves, weighed up the risks and rewards and concluded it's the right way to go – for you.

This section of the book is full of tips on preparing yourself properly, and if you read them all and take my advice, you should find yourself with a clear plan for moving ahead.

Get some help from:

- My book '**Property Investment Success**', which looks at the pros and cons of traditional pensions and makes the case for property as a robust investment vehicle.
- A financial advisor or wealth manager who understands property investment – preferably one who invests in property themselves.

....

"An investment needs to make sense today and tomorrow.'

Robert Kiyosaki

Tip 3

Read property and business books

Knowing your subject is one thing; reading around your subject is another, and you need to keep your eyes wide open on your property journey.

Make no mistake, property investment is a business and, if you want to be truly successful, you need to treat it that way. You have to be prepared for the peaks and troughs that every business goes through, especially in its infancy, and understand business fundamentals.

Before I started investing, I read pretty much all the books that are considered 'the classics' by most property investors. That list includes:
- 'Rich Dad, Poor Dad' by Robert T. Kiyosaki
- 'The Dip' by Seth Godin
- 'The Millionaire Next Door' by Thomas J. Stanley
- 'Think and Grow Rich: The Original Classic' by Napoleon Hill

...and these are the ones I suggest you start with.

Read biographies of successful entrepreneurs, regardless of the field they're in, because you'll learn a huge amount about what it takes to be successful in business and life. Read about different types of property investment - even if you're only planning to buy a couple of single-let starter homes, you never know where that might lead. Read about investment, read the business section of the newspapers, read about overcoming adversity, read case studies and success stories….. read as much as you can, you'll always learn something.

And that's the point: you must never stop learning. Always look for advice from those who have been there and done it, and be open to new ideas.

Get some help from:

* Free sample chapters from my other books: just go to **nickfox.co.uk** and click on FREE STUFF.
* The Amazon Best Sellers list - look in the Business & Money category.
* Other investors – ask them to recommend things they've read.

………………………………………………..

"Whether I'm at the office, at home, or on the road, I always have a stack of books I'm looking forward to reading."

Bill Gates

Tip 4

Set some personal goals

Getting clarity on what you want from your financial investment is one thing, but you also need to set personal goals. It's been proved that we have a much better chance of success if we're emotionally invested in our ventures, so make sure you tie your money-making plans to something that will make a real difference to you and your family.

The important thing with goals is to write them down and make yourself accountable to them. You might have heard people talk about the acronym SMART and it certainly helps to follow it to make your goals:

- Specific – the more detailed, the better
- Measurable – you must be able to chart your progress
- Attainable – make sure they're realistic
- Relevant/Rewarding – you've got to benefit from them
- Time-bound – set deadlines.

And you must revisit your goals – I reassess mine on a weekly basis to make sure I'm on track. Like lots of people, I also have 'vision boards' around my home and office, with pictures of the things I want to achieve, because we tend to get what we focus on most often. So do whatever helps you keep your goals at the forefront of your mind and use them to drive you forward.

Get some help from:

- The 'Downloadable Templates' section of my website, **nickfox.co.uk**, where you can get a couple of goal setting document templates.
- MindTools.com – it has lots of great tools to help you not only set goals, but also manage your time, make decisions, manage project, etc.
- 'Goals' by Brian Tracy and 'Goal Mapping' by Brian Mayne. They're two of the most commonly recommended books on goal setting and there's a reason why!

………………………………………………..

"People with goals succeed because they know where they're going."

Earl Nightingale

Tip 5

Examine your finances

If they're honest, most people would probably say they have a fair idea of their finances, but couldn't actually tell you their net worth or how much they make every month from earnings and investments, after costs and expenses.

Those are just some of the things you need to know about your own financial position before you start investing in property. Think of yourself as a company and examine your finances in the same way you would analyse any business's books.

It's not that hard – you just need to be organised with your information and keep on top of your assets, income and outgoings. There is software you can get hold of, but you can manage perfectly well with a spreadsheet.

Once you have a clear picture of your own cash flow and profitability, you can then start to work out how much you're going to need from your investment, and by when.

Get some help from:

- The free 'personal financial snapshot' that you can

download from my website. Go to **nickfox.co.uk** and click on 'FREE STUFF'.

- Your accountant, if you have one. They should be able to help you pull together the key figures on your finances fairly easily.

....

"If you make time each month to give your money some attention, you'll start the next year in fabulous financial shape."

Suze Orman

Tip 6

Understand good debt vs bad debt

Borrowing money is not a bad thing. Quite the reverse; all very successful businesspeople have a lot of debt. That's not because they don't have the money themselves, it's because they appreciate that using other people's money is very often the wisest financial move.

Good debt is borrowing that doesn't cost you anything. It's using money from the bank or another 3rd party to make an investment that (1) makes enough money to cover the cost of the debt and (2) grows in value or gives income over and above that. You're making money with other people's money.

Bad debt is what gets too many people into trouble. It's borrowing – often on credit cards – to buy depreciating assets or pay for holidays and other entertainment. And this bad debt needs money from your wage packet to pay back both the borrowing and the interest it accrues. In short, the cost of repaying the debt reduces your income.

Borrowing to build a property portfolio, rather than tying up your own money, is usually the most sensible option – IF you've done your research and invest in properties that are growing in value and/

or producing income at the right level. That way, you're getting the market and your tenants to pay for your debt!

Get some help from:
- Robert Kiyosaki's richdad.com. All 'Rich Dad' material talks about good & bad debt, so you can't go wrong!

…………………………………………………………………..

"Be careful when you take on debt. If you take on debt personally, make sure it is small. If you take on large debt, make sure someone else is paying for it.

I use debt to buy assets. Most people use debt to buy toys and liabilities."

Robert T. Kiyosaki

Tip 7

Appreciate what leverage can do for you

To really understand good debt in property investment, you need to understand leverage and appreciate the huge benefits of borrowing via mortgages.

As with any financial investment, it's all about returns. The easiest way to illustrate this is with an example, so let's assume you're buying a property costing £100k and the market then grows by 10%. Your £100k becomes £110k and you've made £10k (less costs, obviously).

Buy with cash:
> £10k profit / £100k investment = **10% return**

Buy with £25k deposit and £75k mortgage, leveraging your purchase with the bank's money:
> £10k profit / £25k investment = **40% return**

You've made the same profit on the capital growth of your property for a quarter of the personal investment. Yes, you've got to pay the interest on your loan, but you're still far better off. And if you're making rental profit each month, that makes it an even greater investment.

Spread your £100k available capital over the purchase of 4 houses instead of just one and suddenly you're looking at £40k capital growth, rather than £10k, plus four times the rental income. You've used leverage to increase your returns.

Get some help from:

- 'Rich Dad, Poor Dad' by Robert T. Kiyosaki. It explains leverage and other basic financial principles very well indeed.
- Google! Search with the phrase 'leverage in property' and you'll find lots of different explanations, case studies and articles about what leverage is and the benefits of using it to buy property.

....

"The most important word in the world of money is cashflow. The second most important word is leverage.... Leverage is the reason some people become rich and others do not."

Robert T. Kiyosaki

Tip 8

Look at interest-only mortgages in a new light

In the bad old days of mis-sold interest-only mortgages, lots of people took them out on their own homes and paid into an endowment policy. That was supposed to grow in value to equal the original amount borrowed so that, at the end of the mortgage term, you'd have paid off the interest as you went along, accrued a lump sum to settle the debt and were left owning your home.

But the endowments and other repayment vehicles didn't grow as they should have and pretty much everyone was or would have been left with a considerable shortfall at the end of the term. Interest-only mortgages suddenly became known as a bad thing.

But that's because people – quite rightly - want the security of knowing they'll own their home. Property investment is different.

When a property is only a wealth-creation vehicle, you're looking at maximising cashflow and profits and aiming to sell it at some point. Owning it beyond 20-25 years is not likely to be a concern; your priority should be making sure that, for the time you hold the asset, it generates as much wealth as possible.

So, if you can reduce your monthly outgoings by only paying the interest on your borrowing (mortgage), rather than repaying any of the capital, why wouldn't you do that? You're still benefitting from all the capital growth on the property, give yourself a better chance of generating income from rent AND you get tax relief on the interest element of any buy-to-let mortgage. In my opinion, it really is a no-brainer.

Get some help from:

- A financial advisor who also invests in property themselves. They'll understand what you're trying to do and be able to explain the benefits and risks of going down the interest-only route.

………………………………………………………………..

"The biggest reason why I buy property is to acquire debt, for the simple reason that the amount of debt stays the same, but the asset against which that debt is secured goes up in value."

Dolf de Roos

Tip 9

Speak to a wealth manager

"A wealth manager helps a client construct an entire investment portfolio and advises on how to prepare for present and future financial needs. The planning function of wealth management often incorporates tax planning around the investment portfolio, as well as estate planning." – Financial Times Lexicon

Some people say they can't afford to pay for the advice of a wealth manager; I say I can't afford not to. They're often thought of as only for the ultra-wealthy, but even if you're only what you might call modestly well off, a wealth manager should be able to save you far more than their fee.

The benefit of using a wealth manager is they specialise in looking at all your financial interests as a whole and providing investment recommendations. Speaking to someone at the earliest stage of your property investment plans means they can help you decide what kind of thing you should be investing in and help you take the most tax-efficient and profitable route.

Too many investors start out without taking any advice on the financial and legal structure of what they're doing and that can be very costly to put right down the line. So book an appointment with a wealth manager and make sure you're on the right track to achieving your goals from the very start.

Get some help from:

- findawealthmanager.com is a good website. Answer a few investment questions and they 'match' you with appropriate wealth management firms in your desired area.
- Properly qualified advisors. Make sure anyone you take advice from holds a Chartered Institute for Securities and Investments (CISI) masters qualification.

....

"Success is a state of mind. If you want success, start thinking of yourself as a success."

Joyce Brothers

Tip 10

Make a plan for your financial future

Setting goals, examining your finances and speaking to a wealth manager or other financial advisor should put you in the position of being able to make a good financial plan.

Your plan should be as detailed as possible and lay out:

1. Exactly where you are now, financially
2. How much money you need and when
3. Your 'end goal'

Write down all the things you need money for, do some research on the cost of those things and factor in inflation (I use an average 3% per annum figure) so that you can put down realistic figures. If you do a draft of this before you meet with a financial advisor, it'll make a good basis for your discussion.

Having this plan will also give you a context for when you start getting specific about investing, because you'll know as and when you need income and capital lump sums and can therefore structure your investments to match those needs.

Again, as with setting personal goals, having a clear, written financial plan should help you stay focused and achieve the financial future you want.

Get some help from:

- My book **'Property Investment Success'**, which has more information on financial planning and makes the case for property as an alternative pension plan.
- The government's moneyadviceservice.org.uk, which has a lot of very useful information and tools to help you plan your financial future.

....

'Already one in three people is opting for a property nest egg as opposed to a conventional pension.'

The Telegraph, November 2014

Tip 11

Have an exit strategy from the start

Ultimate success in property investment comes from how well you manage the process of getting money out of your asset. Even if ongoing income from rent was your primary focus, you will almost certainly be looking to sell at some point and swap your property for cash.

Even if you plan to hold property and eventually pass it on to your children, you should always have a Plan B in case you need to release the equity...because you just never know when circumstances might change and you might need to access your capital.

And the most important reason for thinking ahead is that property – particularly if you have a sizeable portfolio – can have enormous tax implications. So it's vital you plan properly with a wealth manager or financial advisor how and when you will dispose of your assets. Your end goal will influence what property you invest in and how you own it.

All that means you need to think about your exit strategy/ies from the very start. You don't want to have to postpone retirement or other plans because your money's tied up or you've ended up with far less wealth than you'd hoped.

Get some help from:

- A wealth manager or financial advisor, together with a property tax expert.
- Talking to other professional investors who are building their wealth through property. Getting an idea of how other people plan to exit will give you a good feel for your options and some food for thought.

....

"Would you tell me, please, which way I ought to go from here? That depends a good deal on where you want to get to."

Lewis Carroll, Alice in Wonderland

Tip 12

Think about both income and capital growth

Sounds obvious, doesn't it? Every investor would love good income and capital growth and knows they're what property can give you. But you need to understand how you get each, and that the chances of you finding a property that delivers well on both fronts are extremely slim.

Properties in areas that tend to grow well and more quickly in value are usually either expensive homes where the mortgage costs are therefore high, or smaller single lets, such as new-build apartments in rapidly-expanding areas. In both these cases, the positive cash flow, i.e. profit, tends to be low. Conversely, properties that generate good profit from rental income tend to be HMOs, which are usually in areas where the market is slow and steady. That's why I say you need to pick your priority.

Each time you make an investment, it should be because it helps deliver on your overall strategy, and that's likely to include a mix of income-generating and capital growth assets. So be clear about when you need to focus on which kind of investment, and consult a property tax expert to make sure that as you're creating wealth, you're holding on to as much of it as possible!

Get some help from:

- My book **'Property Investment Success'**, which explains the variety of income-producing, short-term growth and long-term growth strategies.

How does your financial future look?

If you haven't reviewed your pension provision for a while or aren't completely happy with how your current investments are performing, take a closer look at property.

In **Property Investment Success**, Nick Fox discusses the pros and cons of traditional pensions and makes the case for property as a robust alternative investment vehicle. He looks at how property can deliver different kinds of returns at different times and shows how you can build a tailored portfolio that perfectly satisfies your own future financial needs.

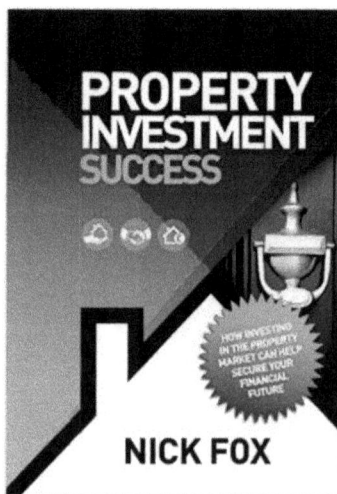

Available now online at **amazon.co.uk** & **nickfox.co.uk**
Books, eBook, Kindle & Audio

Tip 13

Understand yields and returns

There are three main reasons why you need to understand what yields and returns are and how to calculate them:

1. So you know whether your investment is working better for you in property than it could be elsewhere
2. To enable you to compare the performance of your properties with both the average market and other investors' properties
3. So you can properly track how your properties are performing and what they're delivering over time.

Yield

This expresses a property's rental income and profit as a percentage of its value. It gives you a good overview of how different properties stack up as cash flow investments before you buy, and it's useful to compare with other investors.

- annual rental income / current property value = gross yield
  - e.g. £30,000 / £200,000 = 15%
- annual rental profit / current property value = net yield
  - e.g. £12,000 (£30,000 - £18,000 costs) / £200,000 = 6%

Do make sure you know whether people are quoting net or gross figures, so you can be sure you're comparing like with like.

Return on investment

This figure lets you see how hard your capital is working for you and allows you to make a comparison with other properties and other types of investment.

- Annual profit / total capital invested = ROI
  - e.g. £12,000 / £50,000 = 24%

Every year, the £50k you invested is giving you a 24% pre-tax return.

Knowing these figures and regularly updating them means you'll stay on top of your investment/s and be able to make changes, if necessary, at the earliest opportunity.

Get some help from:

- Your financial advisors. Have regular meetings – every 6-12 months – to review how your properties are performing.

....

"If you can't measure it, you can't manage it."

Robert Kaplan

Tip 14

Understand the different types of property investment

Property is – in my opinion! – the best wealth creation vehicle, because it's such a flexible asset class. A lot of people come into property with a focus on single-let or multi-occupancy buy to let, then as they go on they learn about the other ways you can make money from property. And now they're doing all sorts: letting, self building, renovating, developing, land deals, commercial lets, sourcing for other investors….

Each type of investment will bring you different returns at different times and it's a good idea to have a mixed portfolio, so you're not over-exposed to a dip in any one sector of the market.

And once you understand all the different ways property can give you a return, you look at every property with multiple paths in mind.

When I'm adding a HMO to my portfolio, I'm not just thinking about how I can configure it to take 6+ tenants; I'm also looking at:
- the size of the plot – is there the potential for development?
- the figures for letting it as a single family home if

the market for multiple-occupancy properties should suddenly dip
- the potential to split it into two properties
- whether there's room to extend and greatly increase the capital value

Get some help from:
- A financial advisor, wealth manager or property tax specialist, who can explain the tax implications of generating profit from each type of property investment.
- Take a look at the second part of '**Property Investment Success**', which looks at how property can deliver different kinds of returns at different times.
- Then read my other books, '**The Secrets of Buy to Let Success**', talking specifically about the options within buy to let, and '**HMO Property Success**,' which focuses on the high-income, multi-let strategy.

....

"One thing I tell everyone is learn about real estate. Repeat after me: real estate provides the highest returns, the greatest values and the least risk."

Armstrong Williams

Tip 15

Start with an investment that gives you some cash flow

It's a well-known saying that in business 'cash is king' and that's certainly true for property investment.

One of the reasons many investors get into trouble is that, regardless of the size of their portfolio, they don't have good enough cash flow. Their investments simply don't give them enough monthly profit to ride out the times when they have void periods, rents fall and interest rates rise – even slightly.

Plus, you need some operating capital for maintenance and periodical improvements and repairs, such as a new boiler, redecoration, new appliances and fixing the roof. If a property isn't generating enough monthly profit to cover all these things and you have to pay out of your own pocket for jobs and subsidise the mortgage payments if you have voids, then you haven't got an asset; you have a liability.

If a property is scampering up in value and you're convinced you can sell in the short to medium term for a good profit, then you might be prepared to keep topping up its coffers in the meantime, but that would be a very risky strategy.

My advice: start with properties that give you a decent profit AFTER the mortgage payment, all bills and allowances for maintenance and voids have been taken into account, plus some has been set aside for the tax bill. And the best income-generating properties in virtually every area are HMOs.

If you have good money-makers as the basis for your portfolio, that gives you the freedom to perhaps cut down on other work while you focus on property – or simply spend more time doing other things! – or build up some working capital to allow you to invest in other ventures.

Whatever you do, don't saddle yourself with heavily-mortgaged properties that only break even on a monthly basis. With no 'wiggle-room', even if you have good equity, you run the risk of being forced to sell before you're ready.

Get some help from:
- 'Rich Dad's Cashflow Quadrant' by Robert T. Kiyosaki. Explains it all brilliantly.
- Chapter 2 of my book '**HMO Property Success**', which looks at the HMO model and discusses the pros (lots!) and cons.

....

"One of the earliest lessons I learned in business was that balance sheets and income statements are fiction, cash flow is reality."

Chris Chocola

Tip 16

Talk to other investors

You can give yourself a really good head start by talking to other people who have already done what you want to. Most people are happy to share experiences and give advice on what worked and didn't work for them, plus they can warn you off some of the cowboys they've come across!

And speaking to landlords and property developers in your area will help you build up a good picture of the local authority's attitude to HMOs and planning. Getting involved in the local landlords association and regularly attending other property networking events will also give you a heads-up on potential forthcoming legislation, infrastructure changes and business ventures that might affect what you invest in and how you let it.

Some networking events are very good; some are dreadful, so don't be afraid to walk away if you don't feel it's for you. My experience is that if you find people keep talking 'at' you and trying to sell you something, it's probably not worth hanging around. It might take a bit of trial and error before you find two or three that suit you, but you'll always learn something – even if it's just what you don't want!

And do remember you should also be playing your part, so make sure you participate and share information, experiences and knowledge yourself – this is a two-way street!

Get some help from:

- The National Landlords Association at landlords.org. uk. They list all the local authorities that work with them and from there you can find out about local meetings.
- The 'investor education' page on justdoproperty.co.uk, which lists all the UK property networking events.
- Me! If you want to know which networking events I rate and which ones I avoid like the plague, contact me via **nickfox.co.uk** for an honest chat!

....

"If you want to go fast, go alone.
If you want to go far, go with others."
African proverb

Tip 17

Find a mentor

A mentor is someone who's achieved the kind of success you want to achieve. They haven't studied property investment; they've invested. They've made mistakes, had highs and lows and come out of it all stronger and more successful – and that's what you want to absorb from them.

Yes, you can forge your own path, but I can absolutely guarantee you, you'll get further, faster, more cost effectively if you ally yourself with someone who wants to help you.

I love being a mentor. Firstly, I get immense pleasure from sharing my experiences and seeing people's delight when they realise how quickly they're gaining knowledge and confidence. And, secondly, it always amazes me what I learn from them.

Mentoring isn't teaching, it's walking beside someone and helping them accelerate their success. And it's a two-way street – you get out what you put in and the more questions you ask, the more information you share about yourself and your goals, and the more you respond to what your mentor is saying, the more you'll get out of it.

Of course, there's a cost involved, but your returns will be infinite. If you want to hear what other people have to say about mentoring, just flip to the back of the book and read some of my clients' testimonials.

Get some help from:

- Your network. As you meet people in the industry, you'll find yourself drawn to personalities that suit your own. Take recommendations from other people, by all means, but trust your gut because you need to trust your mentor.
- **Nick Fox Property Mentoring**. Head to my website at **nickfox.co.uk** and read about what I offer, then if you like what you see, contact the office and arrange to have a chat with me.

....

"The delicate balance of mentoring someone is not creating them in your own image, but giving them the opportunity to create themselves."

Steven Spielberg

Tip 18

Go to shows and exhibitions well prepared

Property shows and exhibitions are great sources of information. You can wander around anonymously, seeing what's on offer and how property investment companies and individuals portray themselves or you can get involved, talk to everyone and ask a million questions.

Book in to listen to seminars – not only will you undoubtedly learn something, but you'll also get a feel for the person giving the seminar, most of whom are professional investors who offer mentoring, investment clubs and services. They're essentially trying to sell their products and services to you, so sit back and see how they do that. Get a feel for what and who is out there.

And shows and exhibitions are also an opportunity for you to compare suppliers: all-in-one utility providers, furniture suppliers, insurance brokers, property managers, etc.

Just make sure you go prepared. Look at the exhibitor list beforehand, note the stand numbers of companies you want to speak to and have some specific questions to ask them. Do some research before the event so that the conversations you have are meaningful and you don't simply get swamped with information. And when you're there, only take leaflets and brochures of things you're actually interested in.

Get some help from:

- The Property Investor & Homebuyer Show, which is held in the spring and autumn each year at ExCel: propertyinvestor.co.uk
- Large conference venues near you. ExCel, the NEC, the SECC, Metro Radio Arena etc. will all have events pages on their websites, so look at what property events they hold each year.
- The NLA and/or your local landlords association should be able to tell you about relevant events.

....

To succeed at any task or ambition, you must mix with like-minded people – learn from their experiences – stand on the shoulders of giants.

Tip 19

Be very wary of anyone selling leads

People who want to sell you leads are doing so for one of two reasons. Either they have an excellent network, built up over a number of years, and are genuinely getting access to excellent deals, but they simply do not have any capital themselves to invest and want to monetise the leads. Or - and you'll come across a lot of these – they want to make some quick and easy money. In this case they have an average network that sources cheap properties to sell on with the promise that they'll grow massively in value and 'wash their face' in the meantime.

These deals are often not checked out properly by the sourcer and why should they bother? They're not going to have to deal with the fallout when it turns out not to be a very good investment – they've had their money and moved on. Potential yield figures they quote will often be gross, not net, and you absolutely shouldn't take their surveyor's valuation or any 'special' or 'exclusive' finance deals they offer you – both are likely to be unreliable. Insist on dealing with professionals you select yourself.

There are some companies that offer leads totally above board and many of their deals are perfectly good investments. But you will pay a fee to access them and they're highly unlikely to be *great* deals.

The long and short of it is, if you're serious about property investment, the very best thing you can do is educate yourself and become an expert at sourcing properties yourself. That way, you can be 100% in control of your investment and build your local reputation as a professional investor. And then there's a distinct possibility people will start to come to you for deals!

Get some help from:

- The Property Ombudsman, tpos.co.uk. All estate agents are required to be registered with TPO, so that buyers have a redress scheme and can be confident they're operating to a code of practice. Anyone introducing a buyer to a seller is deemed to be an estate agent, so only deal with sourcers who are members of TPO – there is a name search facility on the site.
- Other investors. People are very willing to dish the dirt on cowboys and usually happy to recommend reputable sourcers, so ask around.

The Estate Agents Act 1979 states that if someone acts on behalf of a buyer or a seller in the sourcing or acquiring of property, they are governed under the Estate Agents Act.

Tip 20

Sign up for e-newsletters and updates

This might not sound very important to you in the grand scheme of things, but signing up for alerts on industry news and legislation can help keep you one step ahead. If you're in the loop on changes that could impact you in the future, you can move to make sure you benefit properly from good news and minimise the impact of anything that could affect you negatively.

Look for organisations, companies and individuals that send out good information and comment on industry news as soon as it's announced. Independent property industry expert Kate Faulkner gives great information and breaks down the jargon in her regular propertychecklists.co.uk newsletters - and if you sign up to receive them, you can also download some very useful checklists for your property projects.

Start by registering for pretty much everything you see, then you'll quickly work out which e-shots are worth hanging on to and which are not helpful. Aim to have between five and ten regularly dropping into your inbox that you know will be interesting and useful to you. You don't want to be swamped, but make sure you're getting updates on everything that relates to you and your business. And sign up for general property market e-shots as well as those specifically on buy to let or investment – you should have an awareness of the whole sector, not just your little corner of it!

Then use the information to help you make decisions that keep your property business up to date and operating at the upper end of the investment market.

Get some help from:

- propertytribes.com and property118.com – they're both sites with good content and send out interesting regular newsletters.
- Rightmove. You can sign up for a personalised monthly newsletter with sales and rental data for your investment area. Go to rightmove.co.uk/property-investment
- Facebook. There are some really good property discussion groups, the best of which I think is 'HMO – Houses of Multiple Occupancy Network (Official)'. It has lots of good property investment information and discusses buy to let legislation changes as soon as they're announced, so join up and get involved.

....

"As a general rule, the most successful man in life is the man who has the best information."

Benjamin Disraeli

Tip 21

Accept there'll be problems

If you go into property investment with the mindset that you're going to be different to everyone else - you're going to do it right, your tenants will be different to everyone else's, you're going to look after your properties so well that you simply won't get the problems other people do – you're in for a shock.

In this business, as in any other, there are things that are simply beyond your control. Yes, you can put checks in place and make sure you, your staff and your team are as good as they can be, but you will still get problems. At some point, a tenant will default on their rent and refuse to leave; someone will cause damage to your property; utility companies and other service providers will let you down.....When you're dealing with so many people, each of whom have different priorities to you and intentions you might know nothing about, things will not always go to plan.

The most you can do is accept that it's entirely normal to encounter problems and make sure you have done as much as you can to mitigate the negative impact of those issues. Make sure you reference check properly; take out the right landlord insurance, including for malicious damage and possibly rent guarantee insurance; communicate well with tenants and fix problems quickly; pay contractors on time, etc.

Then budget for the problems. When you do your figures, factor in void periods, keep an amount aside for maintenance and repairs, allow for the fact that you might need to engage an eviction specialist once every few years. In short, don't be surprised.

Get some help from:

- 'The Dip' by Seth Godin. It gives you an excellent overview of the kind of lows you can expect in your property business.
- Your mentor. Share everything with them, good and bad – that's what they're there for.
- Other investors. There is no problem you could come across that another investor hasn't already come across and dealt with. So never be afraid to ask for help and advice.

"In investing, what is comfortable is rarely profitable."
Robert Arnott

Tip 22

Put a value on your time

I speak to a lot of investors who tell me they're saving money by looking after their properties themselves. They do most of the maintenance themselves, they find and manage the tenants and they do their own bookkeeping and accounts. As a result, they say, their properties are more profitable than if they paid someone else to do all these jobs that they can easily do.

But all that takes time and effort and how much is your time worth? What else could you be doing with your time? What do you earn per hour doing your day job? How much is time spent with family and friends worth to you? Are you really making the best use of your time by tackling these jobs yourself?

For me, it's absolutely not worth it. If I can pay someone anything up to £20 an hour to complete any task, it's a no-brainer. That's because I can earn more than that from concentrating on finding new investments, mentoring or working on some other aspect of my business. Not only that, but even if I'm simply spending time with my kids or my partner, that's worth far more to me than £20 an hour.

When you watch property programmes on television, you often see couples who run themselves into the ground for a year, 18 months, tackling most of a project themselves, then telling you they've made £30k on the property. Were the hours they put in worth only £15k a year each? If they worked out their hourly rate, what would it have been? Could they have spent that time doing the thing they're actually trained for and earning far more? In the vast majority of cases, undoubtedly.

Not only that, are you actually qualified and skilled enough to do the thing you're tackling, or could someone else do it twice as well in half the time? My golden rule is: if it's not a strength, outsource it. Why spend time trying to improve on a weakness instead of using that time to improve on a strength?

So don't just look at a cost as a cost – put a value on it.

Get some help from:

- elance.com – a directory of freelancers for a variety of jobs.
- fiverr.com – a great site where people advertise their services, a bit like Gumtree for work!
- virtualpa.co.uk – offers virtual admin and PA services, such as answering phones on behalf of you/your company, typing and diary management.

....

"If you don't value your time, neither will others.
Stop giving away your time and talents.
Value what you know & start charging for it."

Kim Garst

Tip 23

Get to grips with technology

If you aren't comfortable with browsing the internet, searching sites and using Google; if you've never used an ExCel spreadsheet and aren't familiar with simple formulae; if you're not good at putting together Word documents; if you can't attach things to emails; if you don't know how to conference call; if you don't do online banking…. you need to start.

Things move quickly in the business world these days and property investment is a business. You might have a bookkeeper and accountant, but if you can't put together a simple budget spreadsheet that you can email to your financial advisor, you're going to lose time and possibly a deal. If you can't use formulae to instantly calculate income, expenditure, yields and returns for every property you're considering buying, you're likely to make a mistake. If you can't quickly check your bank account and make immediate payments – including from your smartphone - you're making life difficult for yourself.

So get some training and practice. You don't have to be able to do anything terribly complicated – you can pay other people to do that – but you really must be able to do what these days are considered 'the basics'. And ever day, the list of 'basics' grows, so get yourself up to speed as soon as possible.

Get some help from:
- Online training courses. A lot of recruitment agencies offer training courses online for Microsoft Office – for example, Reed has a 10 hr course for £49.
- findcourse.co.uk
- Your local college or community centre. Almost every local centre runs courses to gain various IT skills.

....

'Banking apps were used 10.5m times a day across the country in March 2015, eclipsing the 9.6m daily log-ins to internet banking services, and both services are still growing rapidly, according to data from the British Bankers' Association.
And services are still changing rapidly. More than 3,000 people have already used the Nationwide Now service, which enables customers to apply for mortgages and other services through a video link with a staff member.'

Telegraph.co.uk, June 2015

Tip 24

Make yourself a home office

This business generates quite a bit of paperwork. You've got all your purchase documents, mortgage paperwork, renovation & refurbishment receipts, contracts, warranties, certifcates, supplier contracts, tenancy agreements, credit check paperwork, inventories….the list goes on, and it's the same for every property you buy. So you need somewhere to file it all.

You might need to lay your hands on something at a moment's notice, so all this filing needs to be accessible and clearly labelled. As the saying goes, 'tidy desk, tidy mind'.

When you're researching properties, you're usually printing stuff out and putting things in piles, therefore having a decent workspace space around you is important. And you'll be making lots of phone calls, which is much easier if you have a quiet place to talk.

If you don't currently have a room that you could use as an office, could you convert part of a garage or build one in the garden? If you're only planning on having one or two properties, you can get away with having just an area of a room that's your workspace, but make sure you have that as a minimum. You'll find it much easier to get on with your business if there's a dedicated space, separate from the rest of your home, and your family will certainly appreciate it – trust me, I'm talking from experience!

And, remember, if you're working from home, you can deduct some of your costs from your tax bill. Speak to your accountant to find out how you can take best advantage of this type of tax break.

Get some help from:

- IKEA – for cost-effective storage solutions.
- 'Working from Home' by Paul Edwards. If you've never worked from home, this is a brilliant little guide to doing so effectively.

"When it comes to organising a workspace, relaxation and comfort aren't the primary goals. Work is about efficiency and productivity... The more neat and logically organised your workspace is, the better you will be at your job."

Peter Walsh

FINDING AND BUYING PROPERTY

Tip 25

Invest close to home

People always want to know where the 'hotspots' are right now. The truth is that areas where prices are rising rapidly and potential returns are the highest are either:

- where it's hard to get mortgages – usually overseas in 'emerging markets' or dilapidated property in the UK in areas that are about to undergo regeneration, or
- highly sought-after neighbourhoods that are always near the top of the house price index.

In both cases, you're almost certainly going to have to invest a very large amount of capital. And where the property is cheap, if you've got in at an early enough stage for the chance to get decent rewards, you're also taking a big risk on the area ultimately performing as hoped. Not to mention that by the time most of us have heard about a hotspot, it's no longer in those early stages and therefore no longer hot!

So forget chasing supposedly brilliant deals around the country or further afield – especially if you're in the early stages of your investment journey. The reality is that you should be able to find good deals within 30 minutes of where you live. (The exception being if you live in the remote countryside.) My experience is that people who have very scattered portfolios, for the most part, aren't making any more money than those who invest heavily in one location.

When your properties are close to home:

- you can easily manage them yourself when you're starting out
- you're on hand if anything goes wrong
- by focusing on one area, you'll become an expert on that area and be able to make good decisions more quickly
- you can network locally and build a reputation that should bring you leads and give you access to the best local professional experts
- you can move on good opportunities as soon as you hear about them
- If all your properties are in the same area it's easier to buy goods and services in bulk and negotiate discounts, and you can use the same maintenance contractors.

Virtually my entire portfolio is in and around Milton Keynes and I know that focusing on this area has enabled me to grow it more quickly and profitably than if I had spent my time trying to check out deal after deal in unfamiliar territory.

Get some help from:

- Your local landlords association. Speak to others there who have larger portfolios and find out where their properties are and what they say about investing locally versus further afield.

Dream big, work hard, stay focused and surround yourself with good people.

Tip 26

Understand what makes a good location

A location is only 'good' if it satisfies your specific investment goals and there are two main things to think about here:

1. the broad long-term appeal of an area that means people will always want or need to live there, and
2. the demand within a location for the type of rental accommodation that will provide the returns you need.

Broadly speaking, a good location will have a strong and/or growing economy. That means shops, schools, varied employment opportunities, excellent transport links and inward investment.

But within that broad definition you then need to look at your specific reasons for investing, because what makes a good location for one investor may not be good for another. If you want to maximise rental income, that's usually satisfied by a slightly different location to one that offers high capital growth, because of the different property types and tenures. And if you're looking for short-term returns, the best could be found in a different spot to one that offers reliable long-term cash flow. And you may only be talking a couple of streets apart – this is why it's so important to know your investment area well.

So take the time to research the local economy and to understand exactly where the demand from your target audience is highest – whether that be short or long-term room renters, couples and families looking to rent whole properties, commercial tenants or buyers…..and so on.

Get some help from:

- The planning department of your local council. You should be able to see plans for the next 5 years or so for new housing and commercial development and may be able to access a lot of it via their online portal.
- If you're looking at multi-lets, letting portals such as easyroommate.co.uk and spareroom.co.uk, where you can see the numbers of people looking for accommodation in an area versus the number of rooms or flats available.
- Local letting and estate agents. Ask them what kind of stock they're always short of, and where demand is consistently high.

....

"The problem with real estate is that it's local. You have to understand the local market."

Robert Kiyosaki

Tip 27

Check local area plans and planning at an early stage

Given that the laws on planning can vary significantly from one local authority to another, and are liable to change relatively frequently, this is something you need to look into before you get too far down the investment road.

There should be two prongs to your investigation:

1. **Local area development plans.** You need to know *what's* likely to be built in the foreseeable future and *where*, because you don't want a construction site to suddenly spring up next to your buy to let and drive tenants away, or for anything to cause the capital value of your investment to fall, such as a commercial building or railway line going in next door. As in the last tip, you also need to be aware of which way the local economy is heading and where the best spots for your chosen type of investment are therefore likely to be – today and ten or twenty years down the line.

2. **Planning laws for change of use of a property and extension/conversion.** I know personally of investors who've only found out after they've bought property

that they can't operate it as an HMO. And that can be a very costly mistake. Similarly, if you can't extend as you'd like or can't convert garages and remove parking spaces as you'd planned, your investment can quickly turn into a financial nightmare.

Although you'll probably need to pay for detailed personal advice, you can usually get broad answers and information simply from talking to a planning officer at the council.

Get some help from:
- Your local planning office.
- Town and Country Planners. They often act as part-time private consultants and an be very helpful if you're intending to carry out a big project.
- Your local property networking event.

....

"The thing I preach constantly is do your research; build your knowledge base. Don't just go into business on a whim or a prayer - and don't think 'I'm an entrepreneur so I have to take risks'. Entrepreneurs don't take risks."

Theo Paphitis

Tip 28

Present yourself as a professional

In this business, like any other, people will form opinions about you quickly. Looking smart and being professional in the way you interact with others is one thing, but I'm talking here about presenting yourself as **A** professional, i.e. a professional property investor.

Even if you're only on your first project, you can still be well prepared and well informed. Rightly or wrongly, property investors are sometimes treated with suspicion, so you must do all you can to show you're serious and truly understand property investment, have integrity and will handle things in a decent and efficient way right from the outset. People want to deal with people like that.

So get your legal and financial advisors in place, make sure you know what the national and local authority regulations for planning and developing are, research the local sales and lettings markets, and be clear on what you want to achieve, why and when.

You might be dealing with agents and vendors who aren't familiar with buy to let or working with investors, so you might need to almost take the lead. Be prepared to have to explain clearly what you're doing and expect questions. An open and honest approach, together with showing you're well prepared, will help move things along smoothly.

Then it's back to the simple stuff. Communicate well and do what you say you'll do, when you say you'll do it. And remember that while this may be business for you, it may be a very emotional time for the people on the other end of your purchase, let or sale, and they will appreciate dealing with a calm and professional person.

You'll quickly find out how important your reputation is, so make sure it's good!

Get some help from:

- Personal development coaching. Even if you feel you're naturally confident and successful in business dealings, it's not a bad idea to take a little outside advice. Good coaches can really help you understand how to get the best results out of people and situations.

....

"Professionalism is like love: it is made up of the constant flow of little bits of proof that testify to devotion and care."

Tomislav Sola

Tip 29

Know what lettings information to look for online

You can find a great deal of what you need online, but do you actually know what you need to know?... There are four key areas you should be looking at:

1. **Rental prices.** And you can use advertised prices for your initial research, because, unlike with the sales market, rental properties tend to let for very close to or at the asking price. Check the difference in rent for type and size of property, as well as location.

2. **Demand.** If you're going to be letting rooms, check out on sites like spareroom.co.uk and easyroommate. co.uk how many people are looking for rooms in your location, versus how many rooms there are available. Ideally, you want to invest where demand greatly outweighs supply.

3. **Averages and trends.** You can find this data via the larger agents, such as LSL Property Services - lslps. co.uk – who produce monthly regional buy to let indices, with information on average rents, yields, returns and arrears. Also, Belvoir's quarterly rental index report – in the 'landlords' section of Belvoir.co.uk

– gives data for each individual county in England, not just each region. And don't only look at the raw data, but also read what the senior people are saying about the market.

4. **Legislation.** You can get information on planning and development rules and regulations from your local authority website and on general lettings regulations from the .GOV.UK website, in the 'Housing and local services' section. Landlordsguild.com also has a good rolling series of articles on new and changing legislation.

The more information you can gather, the more detailed you will be able to make your ultimate analysis of an investment. You'll also be able to have more valuable conversations with agents, investment professionals and other landlords.

Do bear in mind, that much of the information will be quite general – in particular, regional data on averages and trends, which can also vary from source to source, depending on exactly how and when they collect it.

So use the internet to help you build a very good overall picture of what your investment could look like, both today and into the future, but then make sure you speak to local industry professionals to fine-tune your plans.

Get some help from:

- The Association of Residential Letting Agents (ARLA) website: arla.co.uk. Useful information for landlords, including monthly reports on the PRS and fairly detailed legislation info.
- Chapter 7 of my book **'HMO Property Success'** on how to research the HMO market.

....

"Research is formalized curiosity.
It is poking and prying with a purpose."
Zora Neale Hurston

Tip 30

Talk to local letting agents

Doing your own research doesn't mean you have to make life difficult for yourself! Yes, of course you should be looking online to see current market rent rates and recently let properties – online research will give you a very good picture of your local market.

But nothing beats speaking to an expert, face to face. Talk to agents that let the kind of property you're considering investing in and ask them about current, historic and likely future demand. Find out what lets quickly, what kind of accommodation they're always short of and what tenants like and dislike. Some of these things will vary from area to area, for example, house sharers in London rate en-suites very highly and in certain areas it's almost impossible to let a room without one, but in Bournemouth they're not bothered. In some areas and for some tenants, allocated parking is essential; in other locations, particularly if you're looking at student lets or other HMOs, it's not important.

Good letting agents that have been established for more than a decade will also know about the local economy and be able to talk to you about trends in demand and types of tenure. Some companies, such as Savills, Belvoir and Your Move, have research and analysis departments and produce their own letting indices, so ask about those. They should also be up to date on legislation and be able to alert you to any potential obstacles you may come across.

Remember, letting agents want your business and will be particularly keen to work with you if you're looking at building a portfolio, so most are very happy to take the time to talk to you.

Get some help from:

- Agents who are members of ARLA, NALS or RICS, so you know they adhere to a code of conduct.
- Rightmove, Zoopla, etc. When you're researching online, make a note of which agents tend to let more of the kind of properties you're looking at investing in and prioritise speaking to those ones.

....

"You are the average of the 5 people you spend the most time with" (Jim Rohn) – so choose carefully!

Tip 31

Look at house price data online

Every investor wants to buy with in-built equity, if they can, which means acquiring a property at less than its 'true' market value. And in order to be sure you're doing that, you need to do some very thorough research into what similar properties in the area have sold for and which way the market is going.

When it comes to negotiating the price for your purchase, it will help if you can arm yourself with some evidence that what you're offering is more realistic than what they're asking (!) and that means collecting relevant data on recent sales and proof of how properties currently on the market are performing.

Most property listing websites and some agents will have a 'sold prices' section, where you can search by postcode and see what's sold nearby and when. Some sites are more helpful than others – Mouseprice, for example, also tells you about similar properties that are currently for sale and gives quite detailed area information, all of which helps you build a picture of your market. For properties for sale, it also has a very handy record of the listing history, so you can see how long it's been on the market, when and by how much it has been reduced in price and if there have been any previous sales that have fallen through.

Remember that both the asking price and any estimates of current value generated by many of these sites are to be treated with caution. They're really no good to you, so focus on historical facts.

Get some help from:
- Rightmove.co.uk/house-prices
- Mouseprice.com

....

"In business, as in life, you don't get what you deserve, you get what you negotiate."

Chester L. Karrass

Tip 32

Find local estate agents that understand buy to let

When you start looking for investment properties, you'll undoubtedly come across some agents who seem deaf to what you tell them. But there are some really good, well-informed agents out there and others who just need a bit of 'encouragement', so don't write them off right away.

If they get the first couple of properties they offer you wrong, explain why they're not suitable and reiterate what you're looking to buy. Take the time to explain exactly what you're doing and, especially if you're intending to renovate/refurbish and reconfigure a property, give them the 3 or 4 key non-negotiables, e.g.

1. Something that could offer 6 bedrooms and I reception room
2. No room that can only be accessed via another bedroom or bathroom
3. An attached garage that can be converted
4. An existing kitchen/diner or a kitchen with potential to knock through.

You'll quickly realise which agents are switched on to what you're looking for and are really trying to find you an appropriate property.

If they keep putting forward things that are totally unsuitable, just because they're in roughly the right area and price bracket, it might be better to move on and find another agent.

It's also good to deal with agents who understand the benefits of selling to an investor who can proceed quickly if necessary or simply be flexible according to the seller's timescale. While the agent is obliged to act in their client's best interest, the best ones understand that it's not all about getting the highest price and, provided they agree with what you're putting forward, should help you make your case to the vendor.

And if they understand property investment, they may be able to offer more tailored letting and portfolio advice. More and more agents are realising it helps their business to be able to provide investors with a fuller service and many have a dedicated research department. So if you have one of these agents in your area, you could develop a very useful and mutually fruitful relationship.

Get some help from:
- Other landlords in your area. Go to local landlord meetings and speak to others who have been buying for some time about which agents tend to be the most helpful.

....

Find the best agents to work with – the ones who take the time to work with you. Together you'll help each other achieve your goals.

Tip 33

Be prepared to look at a LOT of properties!

When you're buying your own home, you might fall in love with the very first property you see, but this is business – and it's a numbers game.

To make a good investment for you, there are a lot of boxes that need ticking: capital input required, permitted planning and development, configuration of the interior, neighbours, plot size, utilities and services, to name but a few. And then, even when you find a property that's right, the vendor might not accept your offer, they may change their mind about selling or the survey could throw up a problem that means it's not worth you proceeding.

A figure I hear quoted by other professional investors is 100:1 – i.e. to find one property that's worth buying, you need to look at 100 sets of details and probably view 10 of those. I'd agree with that, but remember that you can't guarantee your offer will be accepted – and I'd say you should expect two in three to be rejected. So you're going to have to look at 2-300 to secure just one.

Now, that's when you're first starting out. As you build relationships with agents and other property professionals, your leads will get better and better and you'll quickly whittle that ratio right down. I now only have to look at around three sets of details to know whether a property's worth viewing. And when I view, I'm already fairly sure I'll make an offer.

Floor plans are on pretty much every brochure these days and you develop a quick eye for where you might be able to take down and put up walls, convert and extend. And with Google Earth and Streetview, you can take a look around the outside without even leaving your house, so by the time you see the property in the flesh, you're really just checking the condition and making sure you haven't missed anything.

But when you're in the early stages of your investment journey, I'd really recommend you look at as many properties as you can. Not only does that help you learn what does and doesn't work for you, but you're also 'training' estate agents to understand what you're after. So trawl the internet, get in the car and look for boards to get a feel for types of properties and locations, and book appointments to view anything that could be right.

Get some help from:

- A checklist. Put together a template of everything you're looking for and when you're viewing properties, make notes and tick things off.
- Several copies of floor plans – especially if you're

planning on turning a property into an HMO. Playing around with layouts can be a messy process, so make a few copies before you start scribbling!

....

"Success is a numbers game: the number of times you take a shot."

Unknown

Tip 34

Be reliable

Reliability is one of the biggest keys to success – in any aspect of life. If you're not reliable, people will be reluctant to deal with you and there's every chance they'll start telling others. It's bad enough if your friends think you're unreliable, but if people in business find they can't rely on you, they simply won't deal with you any more.

If you tell someone you'll call them back, call. If you tell an estate agent you'll view a property on their recommendation, without seeing details, make sure that's what you do. When you say you'll make a decision by the end of the day, don't leave it until the next day. If you can't make a deadline or an appointment, let people know as soon as possible, and if you've told tenants someone will be there to fix their heating problem within 24 hours, you'd better make sure someone is there.

Generally speaking, people don't mind if you can't do exactly what they want, when they want you to. What they can't bear is uncertainty and constant disappointment.

And although a property purchase might only be a business transaction for you, remember that for the person selling, it's likely to be a large personal financial transaction with significant emotional weight, so it's very important they feel they can rely on their buyer.

So always do what you say you'll do, when you say you'll do it, and get yourself a reputation for being reliable.

Get some help from:

* Your financial and legal advisors. Make sure you've got a good team behind you that will enable you to keep to whatever verbal and written commitments you've made.

....

"Don't be reliable only when it is convenient."

Unknown

Tip 35

Know all your costs

Costs are clearly a big factor in property investment. They can make the difference between turning a profit and not, so it's absolutely vital that (1) you're aware of everything that takes money away from your rental income and (2) you work with accurate figures. So take the time to get together a comprehensive list so you're not surprised – or disappointed - down the line.

First, you've got your initial purchase, renovation and refurbishment costs. Then, assuming you're buying to let, you've got regular mortgage payments, bills and maintenance costs directly associated with the property. They're the obvious ones.

After that, there are your operating costs/overheads, such as the premises you work from, office supplies and equipment, staff salaries and external management costs. You've also got phone and vehicle costs from the running around and communicating you do as a landlord. You might have licensing to pay for, membership of landlord associations, education tools (such as this book!). And you've also got on-going professional services and advice, such as a bookkeeper, accountant and wealth advisor. Many of these will be tax deductible, but they're still costs.

And don't forget the tax bill…

Then you should add in a contingency of 10% for unexpected costs. It doesn't need to be a big figure (assuming you've calculated everything correctly!), but you don't want to take what you think is profit and then suddenly get hit with a large bill you can't afford.

Finally, a big cost that far too many people leave out is the price of their own time. You may think you're saving money by tackling smaller maintenance jobs yourself or doing your own bookkeeping, but could you be earning more than you're saving by using that time more productively?

And you'll find, as you navigate your way around the property investment industry, that when yields and returns are quoted, costs are far too often either left out or very grey. So if headline figures seem high and other people appear to be making way more than you, look at the costs they're deducting. Chances are, they won't all be there.

Get some help from:
- A mentor. This is just one of the areas where they will save you a whole load of time and effort.
- An accountant or financial advisor who invests in property themselves.

....

"Before anything else, preparation is the key to success."
Alexander Graham Bell

Tip 36

Build a viability spreadsheet

I'm a big fan of spreadsheets. If you get a template right at the start, it'll save you loads of time later, when you need to get immediate answers to financial questions.

It's important you're able to quickly establish whether a property investment stacks up as you need it to, so what you want is a spreadsheet on which you can change a few key figures and see what difference that makes to your ongoing profitability, yields and returns. That 'snapshot' will then allow you to quickly and easily compare one investment with another and see how your property is performing against local and national averages and other investment vehicles.

It needs to show all your income and expenditure, together with details of the property value, capital investment and mortgage repayment amount. You must also make sure you include allowances for voids and maintenance and put in a small contingency.

When you're starting out, put as much detail as you can into it. It's a good idea to break down renovation and refurbishment costs in detail on separate spreadsheets and just include headline figures on your main worksheet. Initially, a lot of the figures will be estimates, but you can firm them up as you go along.

Once you've got all the financial elements down, use formulae to calculate the three main performance indicators:

- Monthly and annual profit
- Gross & net yield
- Gross & net annual return

Trust me, you'll find it an invaluable tool for many years.

Get some help from:

- Chapter 2 of my book **'Renovation and Refurbishment Success'**, which goes into some detail about preparing yourself financially.
- The 'Downloadable Templates' section of my website, at **nickfox.co.uk**, where you can purchase an HMO viability analysis template.

....

"If it cannot be measured, it cannot be managed."

Peter Drucker

Tip 37

Don't forget to factor in voids

Voids are probably the biggest potential cash flow killer for landlords. Voids are any period of time when there isn't a paying tenant in your property and they're almost impossible to completely avoid.

There may be time between one tenant moving out and the next moving in, simply for logistical reasons. You might actually want a few days between tenancies in order to carry out some maintenance. You could be let down by a tenant at the last minute and find your property unexpectedly vacant. It may be a tricky time of year – for example, your current tenant might have given notice to leave on 31st December and you simply can't find a tenant who wants to move in over the New Year period. What I'm saying is, often voids are beyond your control.

On the other hand, if you don't do all you can to make your property appealing to tenants, voids could be your fault! Perhaps you've allowed it to become a little dated and there are 'nicer' properties available. Perhaps you're being unrealistic with the rent, or maybe you didn't carry out inspections during the last tenancy and it's going to take some time to clear up the mess made by the outgoing tenants.

Long and short, there are a lot of reasons why you might end up with voids, so you need to budget for them within your costs, so you're not over-estimating the profit you'll end up with. The average void (according to Paragon Mortgages research) over the past couple of years has been between 2.5 and 3 weeks a year, so I'd suggest a 5% allowance is about right.

Get some help from:

- The 'Downloadable Templates' section of my website **nickfox.co.uk**, where you can get hold of a viability spreadsheet, listing all the costs you should take into account, including voids.

....

"In any one year, up to 60% of landlords face void periods, however, only 12% of these take this into account when assessing the ongoing health of their property portfolio. This means a staggering 88% aren't acknowledging the impact this has on their rental income."

Platinum Property Partners, April 2015

Tip 38

Use net figures, not gross

This is a simple point, but one you need to be very aware of, because the two can be wildly different.

In its most simplistic form, a net figure in property investment has had all related costs deducted. The most common figures quoted are for yield and returns, and you need to be clear on whether those figures are net or gross, so that you can compare like for like. Some people only quote gross figures; some call them net when the only cost they've actually deducted is the mortgage repayment; some don't even state whether it's a net or gross figure.

In my opinion, gross figures are almost meaningless when you're talking about the profitability of an investment, not least because your costs could potentially wipe out all your profit.

Look at the difference in net and gross figures in this example:

Purchase price	£200,000
Total capital invested	£75,000
(deposit, buying costs, refurbishment, furnishing, etc.)	
Annual rental income	£30,000
Annual costs	£18,000

Annual profit / net income	£12,000
Gross yield	**15%** (£30k ÷ £200k)
Net yield	**6%** (£12k ÷ £200k)
Gross return on capital	**40%** (£30k , £75k)
Net return on capital	**16%** (£12k ÷ £75k)

In short, the gross figure only tells you how well the rental income stacks up, against a property's purchase price or against the amount of capital you've had to invest. The net figure tells you the important fact: how much money you're actually making - pre-tax, of course.

Get some help from:

- nickfox.co.uk – if you want clarification on this, or need some help, just contact me and my team.

....

"Your net worth to the world is usually determined by what remains after your bad habits are subtracted from your good ones."

Benjamin Franklin

Tip 39

Factor in interest rate rises

Things are pretty good for us at the moment (in 2016), in terms of interest rates. The Bank of England has kept the base rate at 0.5% for six years now, which has been reflected in relatively low mortgage rates, and anyone who had a tracker in place before the credit crunch has been laughing. But at some point in the not-too-distant future, that base rate will go up.

And when mortgage rates go up, the increase in repayments can start to make quite a dent in your income. In the worst case, an increase in an investor's mortgage rate could take them from turning a small profit to having to subsidise their investment every month. And if you have a sizeable portfolio that's ticking along and 'washing its face' at the moment, if every property were to flip into a negative cash flow situation, that could have serious financial implications for you.

So you must plan ahead. There's every chance that rates could rise by 2-3% over the next 5 years, so work your figures based on that and look at what effect each increment of half a percent would have on your profits. Then check to see where your break-even point would be, i.e. what level would a mortgage rate have to hit for you to be *just* staying the right side of the profit/loss line.

Even if capital growth is your priority, I'd say that if you have to subsidise an investment on an ongoing basis - no matter how small the amount is – it's probably not a worthwhile place to put your capital. I like to have an interest rate buffer of an absolute minimum of 5% on any property I buy to hold, and the vast majority of my portfolio could withstand rates climbing to much higher levels.

Get some help from:

- Your financial advisor or wealth manager. They should be able to quickly calculate the impact of various scenarios.

....

"Last week, in a report on the financial stability of the UK [the Bank of England] warned that six out of 10 buy-to-let landlords could be vulnerable if interest rates rise by 3%."

The Guardian, 12th December 2015

Tip 40

Keep a cash reserve

I once heard a couple of so-called 'property gurus' tell a room of investors that they should keep a third of their capital accessible in a rainy-day fund.

While I think that's excessive, and that if you've done your homework and are a professional investor, you shouldn't need anywhere near that amount sat in a bank account doing nothing for you, it's wise to keep some of your money liquid.

Although you can – and should – make proportional allowances in your budget for maintenance and repairs, you might not necessarily have the whole amount needed for a larger job right at the time you need to pay the invoice. You may have to subsidise mortgage payments or cover legal costs initially if you have to evict a non-paying tenant. Compliance with a change in letting laws, planning or building regulations might mean incurring costs you hadn't anticipated. And sometimes boilers all go at once.

So having a cash buffer to fill in the gaps and enable you to get things done when they should be, without causing you pain, is a very good idea. I'd recommend putting aside £5,000 per property, or at least 6 months' worth of easily accessible cash, for those times when the ongoing cash flow can't quite make meet costs - and don't be tempted to dip into it!

Get some help from:
- Your financial advisor. They'll be able to recommend where it's best to keep this reserve – perhaps in premium bonds or in an instant-access savings account.

....

"Always remember, your focus determines your reality."

George Lucas

Tip 41

Understand true BMV

Thankfully, the number of self-styled 'property gurus' and property investment companies headlining their services with promises of 'X% BMV' deals has dropped from the heady pre and early credit crunch days. The concept was right; the methodology was all-too-often less than professional.

'Below market value' as a term is part of the problem. What does it actually mean? What is the market value of a property? Is it the advertised price, the price someone will pay for it (which can vary greatly, depending on how much someone wants a property and how they're buying it), or is it what a surveyor says? Far too many so-called BMV deals are simply cheap properties - and why are they cheap? Often because nobody else wants them!

Remember as well that buying BMV isn't necessarily what it's all about. Yes, we'd all prefer to get hold of a property for less than it's really worth, but if something is going to kick out amazing cash flow, you might be prepared to pay the full asking price if that's what it takes. Do your research and make sure what you're buying really is a good investment.

So, what I call 'true' BMV is below surveyed value. Assuming you're buying with a mortgage, the surveyor's valuation is the only one that counts. Always instruct your own survey – even if one has already been done - and make sure it's carried out by an independent surveyor who's a member of the Royal Institution of Chartered Surveyors (RICS), so you know you can rely on it.

Of course, it's likely you'll have made an offer before you instruct a surveyor, so make sure you do some really solid research into sold house prices in the immediate vicinity. The more properties you analyse and the more you acquire in one area, the better you'll get at assessing a property's intrinsic value.

Once you're sure of how much it's worth in a reasonable market, aim to buy it for at least 15% less than that. That will give you immediate in-built equity and a cushion against prices falling. (See Tip 52 for how to ask for a discount.)

Get some help from:
- Rightmove and Mouseprice for sold house price data.
- Ricsfirms.com to search for a RICS surveyor in your area.

"Only loss teaches us about the value of things."
Arthur Schopenhauer

Tip 42

If buying at auction, make sure your money's in place

Good old daytime property programmes on TV have really boosted the profile of property auctions over the past decade. The bad news for investors is that this means you're now competing with more investors and more homebuyers who, because they're likely to be emotionally attached to a property, tend to bump up the prices.

Still, it is possible to get hold of a bargain at auction, but you've got to make sure you're prepared. And a big part of that is having the money to buy the property in the first place.

When the hammer falls, the property is yours – you've committed to buy – and a deposit of 10% of the purchase price is payable to the auction house right away. This has nothing to do with the deposit you've agreed with your mortgage company – that's a separate transaction you're making with them. The remaining 90% must be paid to the auction house within 28 days.

This means you must know what you're willing and able to pay for a property well in advance and make sure you have sufficient funds immediately available. It also means you've got to have made arrangements with a lender – and that may be a specialist lender - in advance of the auction.

The downside of this is that you will need to pay out some money before you even begin bidding. The mortgage company may ask for fees in advance and you'll have to pay for a survey as well, in addition to any other fees for investigations into the property.

Get some help from:
- The internet! There are lots of very reputable sites with information about the auction process.
- Needless to say, your financial advisor should be able to either help you himself, or recommend a specialist.

....

'Overall lots offered and lots sold were both up 17% and 24% respectively [on November 2014], whilst the total raised at auction grew significantly to £271.9m - up 63%.'

Essential Information Group director, David Sandeman, December 2015

Tip 43

Check property investment companies with Companies House

This is just a short tip, because the heading pretty much says it all!

If you haven't used the Companies House website before, it's pretty easy to navigate. For any Limited Company, you can see:
- When it was incorporated
- A list of the Directors
- Details on when accounts were last filed and if they're overdue
- Copies of abbreviated accounts
- Any changes to details of share allocation, Directors and addresses
- Any dissolutions, strike offs, etc.

…and more.

You can also search under a Director's name, so can see what other companies they're associated with.

Essentially, the website can help you build a picture of how stable and reliable a company or person is and confirm registered addresses, which you can then check out in person, if you so wish. Personally, I'd be a little hesitant about working with someone who had been associated with numerous companies that had all been dissolved or a company whose accounts were overdue. Do bear in mind there could be perfectly reasonable explanations for these things, but it gives you some foundation for asking further questions before getting involved with a person or organisation that promotes themselves as 'experts'.

Get some help from:

- GOV.UK/get-information-about-a-company
- The final section of Chapter 5 in my book **'The Secrets of Buy to Let Success'**, which talks about buying from a investment agent or consultant.

....

Forewarned is forearmed!

Tip 44

Trust your instincts

Another short tip, which comes with a caveat: also do your research. You certainly can't cruise through property investment on instinct alone, but if something feels wrong, question it.

Property is a people business and I'm a big believer in trusting my instincts when it comes to people. Most of us can tell when someone's trying a little too hard to sell something; when they're trying to steer us toward or away from something; when they're not being entirely truthful; when the look of something isn't matching what you're being told about it; when, despite reassurances, we don't feel sure…

So don't be afraid to hold back, ask more questions and even pull out of something if your instinct tells you it's not right. I speak from experience when I say that there are few things worse in business than ending up in a bad situation and saying to yourself, "I knew I shouldn't have done this."

Get some help from:
- A personal development coach. Getting some outside perspective on your own instincts and natural reactions can be incredibly helpful.

"Instinct is a marvellous thing", mused Poirot. "It can neither be explained nor ignored."

Agatha Christie, 'The Mysterious Affair at Styles'

Tip 45

Buy new build late in the day

Housebuilders have three 'pressure points':

1. Right at the start, they need to sell the first few units so they can start marketing their development with 'sold' signs against some of the key properties to generate more interest

2. At the end of the tax year, they need to look as profitable as possible

3. When there are only a few units remaining in a development, it's the pure profit end of the project, so they can afford to take a bit of a hit on the price if it means getting money back in the bank.

So, if you're looking at a new build, try to negotiate at one of these times – and I'd suggest the end of the project is where you'll have the most negotiating power. By then, the best units have been sold and, because the project's complete, there's no opportunity for buyers to select the finishes themselves. The developer is often left with stock they know they're highly unlikely to achieve the asking price on.

At the end of a project, speed of transaction is also very appealing to developers, so if you can assure them the purchase will go through quickly, you should be able to negotiate a discount.

Get some help from:

- Property investment shows and events. Ask any housebuilders or new build agents about any projects coming to an end – you might be able to pick up a bargain, or at least find out some information about when they're going to need to shift stock.

....

"Have no fear of perfection – you will never reach it."

Salvador Dali

Tip 46

Use an experienced buy to let mortgage broker

A lot of the clients I mentor tell me that they already have a mortgage broker they've used for years and that they trust them completely. That's great, but how much experience do they have with buy to let mortgages?

Buy to let is a different ballgame to homeowning and the mortgage aspect often demands a particular approach, especially if you're investing in HMOs, which can limit you to HMO-specific products. And, because buy to let lending is mainly calculated on a rental income v mortgage repayment ratio, it's wise to have a broker who's used to making and supporting applications on that basis.

So there are two things to remember here:
1. Make sure your broker is independent and can access every mortgage product in the marketplace, to ensure you're getting the 'best', i.e. most appropriate deal for your circumstances, and
2. Use someone who has a number of other buy to let clients and who is experienced in obtaining the kind of mortgage you're looking for. While any independent broker is able to act for you from a regulation

perspective, the process should be quicker and less onerous if they're familiar with it.

As with most things in life, following the advice of an expert – someone who's doing a particular job or performing a specific task on a regular basis – means you stand the best chance of getting the best results.

Get some help from:

* Me and my team at Nick Fox Property Mentoring. We're always happy to make recommendations if you need help tracking down a good professional advisor. Call the office on 01908 930369 or email hello@ nickfox.co.uk
* Thebuytoletbusiness.com – an independent brokerage run by people who invest in property themselves. Not a bad place to start if you're looking to discuss some options.

....

"Experience is the teacher of all things."

Julius Caesar

Tip 47

Stick to your figures

This is a simple rule and one that, put simply, governs what you buy. When you're buying a home for yourself, you might have an upper limit that you can't afford to go over, but when you fall in love with a property, you might be prepared to pay more than it's worth, strictly speaking. That can't, or shouldn't happen when you're investing.

A property is only worth buying if it can generate the returns you want and/or need. Do your research, make sure you take into account all the costs, make realistic and evidence-based decisions on the rental income and capital growth you can expect, make allowances for voids, expenses and periodical capital outlays and put it all into a spreadsheet.

Then analyse and assess all the figures to calculate the yield, return on capital and profit. What you're looking for is something that's going to generate money for you when you need it to AND that beats the average for the area.

You'll end up with a purchase price figure that you can't go above, because (a) then the property would no longer generate the returns you need, and/or (b) your research suggests that it's genuinely not worth any more than that.

So don't let yourself be persuaded that just another five or ten thousand would clinch it. Stick to your guns. This is a financial investment, nothing more, so while it might mean that you don't get one property, don't worry – there'll be another one!

Get some help from:

- The 'Downloadable Templates' section of my website **nickfox.co.uk**, where you can get hold of a spreadsheet that will help you analyse all your figures.

....

"An investment operation is one which, upon thorough analysis, promises safety of principal and an adequate return."

Benjamin Graham

Tip 48

Don't overstretch yourself

There are two prongs to this: financial and personal.

Financially, your investment has to make sense. If you over-leverage or tie up money that you might need to access down the line for yourself or your family, it could make life difficult and stressful. You should also take professional advice about how to buy and own the properties you add to your portfolio. Taking out too many buy to let mortgages, for example, could affect your future ability to borrow.

And personally, you might have to work hard for the first year or two, but don't run yourself ragged. This process is supposed to enhance your life and give you a level of financial freedom, so you must make sure it doesn't end up being a milestone round your neck. I know of people who have remortgaged their own house to release capital to invest and then, when the investment's gone wrong, they've been on the verge of losing their home.

Delegate where you can, make use of professional services, etc., as your portfolio grows. You might think you're saving money and keeping a tight rein on your property business by doing much of it yourself, but, trust me, the majority of what needs doing on a day-to-day basis can be handled by someone else – and you might find their abilities for certain tasks outshine yours!

And then there's the whole idea of debt. Building a property portfolio, you can very quickly acquire a lot of debt and unless you're comfortable with that, you could end up having sleepless nights. Just because someone says it's a good financial move to buy more property, that doesn't mean you should go ahead if you're at all unsure.

There will always be good investment opportunities around, so don't overstretch your finances, your physical self or your emotional self if you're not ready or able to make an investment today.

Get some help from:

- Your financial advisor. Make sure you're buying and holding your investments in a balanced way.

....

"Good debt is a powerful tool, but bad debt can kill you."

Robert Kiyosaki

Tip 49

Don't wait for the best deal

Once you've done all your research and run a load of figures, you'll know what the ideal property investment would look like. Then you need to accept that you might never get it.

Some people call this idea 'analysis paralysis' – where you're so caught up in trying to learn everything you can about an investment and finding a better deal than the one you're looking at, you never get off the starting blocks.

You've got to take the plunge at some point, so just accept that your first purchase is simply going to be 'good'. As long as you've made a good job of putting your figures together and given yourself enough breathing space in case things don't quite go 100% to plan, then as long as a property meets those carefully calculated minimum requirements, there's no reason not to buy it.

When you're starting out, it's often a question of confidence, rather than money, so ask for help if you're not sure whether you're making the right decision. This is where having a mentor can really help – someone there by your side who can reassure you that you're making the right decision.

And there'll *always* be a better deal somewhere, so don't beat yourself up because you've made an investment that's not the absolute best it can be. As you gain experience, you'll learn and improve on the quality of your property projects and fine-tune what would make a deal better for you.

Remember, if your money is invested in something that's generating a good return, that's better than it being sat in the bank doing nothing or in another investment that's not doing very well. There's no such thing as 'the best deal', just better deals. And that's something you can and will work on.

Get some help from:

- Me and my team at Nick Fox Property Mentoring. We're here to help people make good decisions, so if you'd like to discuss how we can help you, call the office on 01908 930369 or email hello@ nickfox.co.uk

....

"Having a vision in mind, a goal let's say, is a good thing. Unfortunately, so many of us are blinded by the greatness of our vision that paralysis and inaction sets in. I try to focus on the individual steps and let them lead one to the next. The vision that eventually appears may not be exactly what you had in mind, but it will be the

right one for you, because you did the work and you took the necessary action."

Charles F. Glassman,

'Brain Drain: The Breakthrough That Will Change Your Life'

Are you looking for a sound investment that can give you both income and growth on your capital, but nervous about the future of the property market? This book will put your mind at rest.

In **The Secrets of Buy to Let Success**, Nick shares his knowledge and expertise about the market, guiding the reader step by step through the basics of building a solid and profitable property business – even through an economic crisis.

If you're completely new to property investment, this book is a great place to start. It carefully explains the market and how you should approach each part of the buy to let process, from financing, through acquisition, to managing your portfolio. Discover the different ways you can let property and how to insulate yourself from the potential pitfalls.

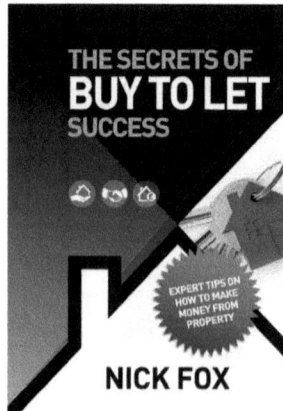

THE SECRETS OF
BUY TO LET
SUCCESS

EXPERT TIPS ON HOW TO MAKE MONEY FROM PROPERTY

NICK FOX

Available now online at **amazon.co.uk** & **nickfox.co.uk**
Books, eBook, Kindle & Audio

Tip 50

Give yourself options

In life, you should try never to find yourself boxed into a corner, and that's certainly true of property.

Property investing should be viewed as a medium to long-term investment and you're likely to be holding the bricks and mortar you've bought for 15-20 years. During that time, some things are highly likely to change - perhaps the type of accommodation tenants are looking for, affordability, local economy and infrastructure, your own personal situation, etc. – and all of those things can impact positively or negatively on your property investment.

You should do all you can to avoid ending up with a property that only benefits you financially in one scenario.

So it makes sense for you to try and buy property that gives you options, for example, something that could relatively easily be reconfigured internally to allow for different types of let or converted from one residence into two. Look for something with a large plot that could be split and developed or sold. If you're building a portfolio that includes commercial property, check whether it could be changed to residential use in the future, if necessary. And invest in different types of property and let, so you don't have all your eggs in one basket.

You should also have a flexible approach to what's included in your tenants' rent. For example, you might want or need to switch from your tenants paying all the bills themselves to an all-inclusive agreement.

And remember that you may need to release your capital at some point, and sell. So think carefully before buying something of a type or in an area that has a very specific market appeal, such as an HMO in a student area or a residential property that's above commercial premises.

Get some help from:

- Chapter 3 of my book, **'Property Investment Success'**, which discusses the different range of options property gives you.

....

In addition to the single and multi-let rental properties I own, I also took the decision to buy premises for my childcare business, rather than renting. As a result, my business pays me rent and I have chosen a property that will also let well as a House in Multiple Occupation, should I move the business in the future.

Nick Fox, 'Property Investment Success'

Tip 51

Double-check everything before you offer

It might sound obvious, but I've know many people who have made an offer on a property, only to have to go back and amend it when they realise they've missed something or other in their calculations.

If you do get your figures wrong, you have two choices: explain what you've done to the agent and submit a revised offer, or live with it. The first could make you look unprofessional; the second could mean the investment is no longer very good. In the worst case, if you've really made a mess of things, you may be left with no option but to pull out and walk away.

None of these is a good situation to find yourself in, so before you make any offer on a property, go back and check you haven't miscalculated or left out any costs.

It's also a good idea to go back and update your research. It may have been a few months since you checked demand for rented accommodation and plans for new accommodation being built in the area, etc., so just make sure everything is still as you believe it to be.

And have a chat with your financial advisor or wealth manager to let them know exactly what you're doing, so that they can make any necessary arrangements for your capital and advise you if there's anything else you should consider before going ahead.

Get some help from:

- The 'Downloadable Templates' section of my website, **nickfox.co.uk.** There's an HMO Viability Analysis template, which is just as useful if you're making any kind of buy to let investment.

....

Check, check, then check again!

Tip 52

Ask for a discount – but don't be insulting!

I've heard a lot of investors saying they never buy anything unless they can get a 25% discount. Frankly, I think that's a daft thing to say. Of course, we'd all like every property we buy to come with 25% in-built equity, but to suggest that if you can't achieve that, you're somehow not doing it right is rubbish.

The key thing to remember is that you'll only get a discount if there's a good reason for a seller not to hold out for more money. In short, their time pressure has to be the most critical thing. That could be:

- They're desperate to release the capital because they're in financial difficulty and they'd rather get most of the equity quickly, than all of the equity at an unknown point
- They're in a chain and the people above them are pushing and possibly threatening to pull out, so they'd rather drop their asking price than lose the home of their dreams
- A relationship has broken down and they want to move on and make a fresh start as quickly as possible
- Someone has died and the beneficiaries of their estate

want to liquidate their assets as soon as they can
- A bank has repossessed a property and, as long as they get their money back, they not too worried about how much they make over and above that…

….and other time-related reasons.

So always make sure you know exactly what a vendor's position is and what they're looking to achieve by selling. If you can offer a good and quick solution to a problem, that gives you reasonable grounds for asking for a discount.

An important thing to remember is that you're building a reputation and don't want to be known as someone who makes silly offers – that's just a waste of everyone's time and could easily be insulting to a vendor, who may decide simply not to deal with you any more.

So offer a fair amount that means both you and the vendor walk away feeling good about the transaction. Think about what they need, look at your figures and research and come up with a sensible offer that makes you look canny and fair, rather than like a chancer.

Get some help from:
- The estate agent. If they're good at their job and genuinely acting in their client's best interests, they'll be able to guide you towards a figure that might be acceptable to the vendor.

"The law of Win/Win says, 'Let's not do it your way or my way; let's do it the best way."

Greg Anderson

Tip 53

Explain your offer in writing

In this business, you'll do well to remember to put/get everything in writing. If something's down in black and white and dated, it can't easily be disputed, plus you can be absolutely clear on what you're doing or saying, and why.

Because your offer is likely to be at an amount below the asking price, it's highly unlikely to be accepted right away. So it'll help a great deal if you can briefly explain why you're making the offer and the benefits of the vendor accepting it.

Make it clear that it's a business transaction for you. The property may be a treasured home for the current owner, so it's often helpful to them to reiterate that your offer is not necessarily a reflection of what the property might be worth to another homeowner; it's simply a figure that makes sense to you, investment-wise. And if you've sought out some comparables – similar properties that have sold recently locally, that support the level of your offer – they may be worth mentioning.

And then sell yourself as a buyer. It's highly likely you'll be able to reassure them your finances have been organised, the purchase is not dependent on any sale, you can move as quickly as the legal and mortgage processes allow, etc. If the vendor has a related onward purchase, it's a good idea to state that you can be flexible time-wise, should there be any hold-ups or problems with that transaction.

Although the agent will issue a memorandum of sale if the offer is accepted, it often adds a weight for the seller if you include details of your mortgage broker and legal representative.

Get some help from:
- The 'Downloadable Templates' section of my website, **nickfox.co.uk**, where you can get hold of an offer letter template.
- Your legal representative. If you're adding in any conditions to your offer, you might want to check what its right to put down at this stage.

"You need to put it all down in writing so everybody is on the same page, everybody understands."
Bill Kennedy

Tip 54

Meet & get to know your surveyor

Building a good relationship with a surveyor who understands what you're doing will prove very useful as you brow your portfolio. It won't change the outcome of what they report, but it should enable you to get the information you need, when you need it. And that will allow you to make informed decisions more quickly.

It can take several days and often weeks to get back a surveyor's report, particularly if you've commissioned a HomeBuyer Report or Building Survey. Most of the time, it'll suit you to complete the purchase as soon as possible, so if you can get an overview of the key findings of the survey on the day its carried out, you can start moving ahead with your plans….or not.

So I'd always recommend meeting your surveyor at the property. Some of them – quite understandably - aren't very keen to have someone peering over their shoulder as they work, so make it clear you'd just like to meet them, have a quick chat and then will let them get on with it and either come back or call once they're done.

Provided you're clear and concise about what your intentions are with the property, what you need them to report on, and respect that fact that they're busy and you're not their only client (!), you should be able to establish a good line of communication with them.

Assuming all goes well, they may well be happy in the future to give you overviews and opinions on properties before you commission a full survey.

And if you're investing in HMOs, it's very useful to have a surveyor who's familiar with what you're doing, knows what you'll need from them, and understands the importance of getting realistic room rental valuations.

Get some help from:

- Ricsfirms.com to search for a RICS surveyor in your area

....

Build the right relationships with the right people and nurture them over time and you'll always have a leg up on the competition.''

Paul May

Tip 55

Have a separate property bank account

It might sound obvious, but there are a lot of people who start off buying property and paying out for the initial professional services and even deposits, using their own personal bank account.

You might not be a limited company, but this is an investment - and potentially a business that you're going to have to account for - and completing your tax returns will be a lot easier if everything related to your properties goes through one dedicated account.

Your accountant will thank you; your bookkeeper will thank you; you'll thank yourself when you have to look back over statements for something.

Rents, holding or administration fees and odd irregular payments are much easier to check on if you don't have to sift through a whole load of personal transactions as well - particularly if you're talking about HMOs, where you can easily have 6 rent amounts per property coming in each month. And if all the income and expenditure, including mortgage payments, is going through a separate property account, it's much easier to keep a handle on your profits and quickly see whether there are funds currently available for maintenance and bigger works.

It's also wise to set up a saver account, where you can put money aside for your tax bill.

You're going to have to keep records of a lot of paperwork and a lot of figures, so anything you can do to make keeping track of them simpler has got to be a good idea!

Get some help from:
- Your accountant or bookkeeper.

....

"Talent without discipline is like an octopus on roller skates. There's plenty of movement, but you never know if it's going to be forward, backwards or sideways."

H. Jackson Brown

Tip 56

Make sure you own your properties in the right way

The more people there are involved in the ownership of your investment properties and the more dependents and eventual beneficiaries of your estate you have, the more important it is that they're legally owned in the correct way.

If you're buying with a spouse or partner/s, you need to speak to your legal representative about whether it's more appropriate for you to own the property as Joint Tenants (if one of you dies, your share of the property automatically passes to the other owner/s) or Tenants in Common (you can decide where your share goes when you die). If you get that wrong at the start, it may be difficult or impossible for you to amend at a later date.

It may be better for you to form a company to own the property. That depends on your personal situation and tax objectives, which you'll need to discuss with a specialist property tax advisor.

From a tax perspective, you need to think about whether the property income and eventual capital gain would push you into a higher tax bracket and whether it might therefore be better, for example, for your spouse to own it and take the income.

You might also want to put a property in your children's name/s, but that needs to be talked through with your wealth manager, property tax advisor and legal advisor, as there could be tax and inheritance issues.

In short, there's a lot to think about before you invest, so take professional advice and make sure the wealth and security you're looking to create ends up where you intend them to.

Get some help from:
- The GOV.UK website has information on joint property ownership

....

"Planning, is bringing the future into the present so that you can do something about it now."

Alan Lakein

RENOVATION, REFURBISHMENT AND GETTING READY TO RENT

Tip 57

Ask a letting agent's opinion

To a certain extent, putting together a buy to let property - or a property to sell, is formulaic. Keep it neutral, make the fittings hard-wearing and modern, etc., etc... But the most important thing to do is make sure your finished product appeals to the kind of tenant or buyer you want it to.

And so, when it comes to buy to let, you need to know the top things that are attracting tenants right now. Spacious and light, hardwearing and neutral, will always be good basic rules, but the extra things that make tenants snap up a property can change, depending on trends and overall expectations, plus needs and wants. Whether and how to furnish, in particular, can vary from area to area and depend on the type of tenant.

Letting agents are dealing with tenants every day, so take advantage of their knowledge and expertise – most will be happy to advise you, in the hope of gaining your business. As well as giving you useful 'inside' information, it's another opportunity for you to see which agents are the most helpful and professional.

So take your plans into agents before you start on the renovation and refurbishment and ask what they think about the accommodation, room sizes and plans for fixtures, fittings and white goods, etc. They're the experts and may come up with some good suggestions or point out things you may have overlooked.

If you're intending to use an agent to let or manage the property for you, ask if they'd mind coming round towards the end of the project, just to check that everything's as good as it can be. If you involve them in the process and they feel they've contributed to the finished home, they'll be more likely to be enthusiastic about marketing it and everybody wins: you get a quick let at the best rent, they get their commission more quickly and the tenant gets one of the best homes on the market.

Get some help from:

- Chapters 7 and 8 of my book, **'HMO Renovation and Refurbishment Success'**, which has a lot of good information about what to do with the interior, as well as photographs of the process and finishes.
- Me and my team at Nick Fox Property Mentoring. We're here to help people make the right decisions, so if you'd like to discuss how we could help, call the office on 01908 930369 or email hello@nickfox.co.uk.

....

"All knowledge is worth having."

Jacqueline Carey

Tip 58

Get to know the neighbours

It's important to consider the neighbours of your investment property from the outset. Unfamiliarity and uncertainty can cause people to jump to conclusions and your neighbours could well have preconceptions about rented properties – particularly HMOs – or have had bad experiences in the past.

I don't mean that you need to become firm friends, but you should be friendly, considerate and approachable.

Before any renovation work begins, knock on the door and introduce yourself to the immediate neighbours. Have a short letter prepared, explaining briefly what's going to be happening at the property, how long the work is expected to last for and that it will then be tenanted. Give them either your contact details and/or those of the managing agent and let them know they can contact you if they have any concerns.

Make sure you remain professional and politely stand your ground if they suggest that you shouldn't be doing what you are, etc. Let them know you've gone through all the correct processes with the local authority and are complying 100% with all legal regulations and requirements.

It's often a good idea to pre-empt any potential disputes or unpleasantness by saying that you'd really appreciate them getting in touch if they think something's not right, as you're a professional landlord and want to be able to address and resolve any issues before they become a big problem.

A nice touch is to drop round a bottle of wine, or other small token once the refurb's complete, to thank them for their patience during works. They won't be expecting it and it should get things off to a good start.

Get some help from:

- GOV.UK has some useful information relating to neighbour disputes.

....

"The social brain is in its natural habitat when we're talking with someone face-to-face in real time."

Daniel Goleman

Tip 59

Employ a project manager

If you've never carried out a refurbishment project, or only ever had a bit of work done to your own home, here's a word of warning: it's most definitely not an easy thing to manage.

You're probably going to be employing a builder, a plasterer, an electrician, a plumber, a decorator and a carpet fitter, and many of the jobs they'll be doing have got to be done in a particular order. Contractors have something of a reputation for being brilliant at blaming each other for falling behind schedule and if you don't know exactly what each of their jobs entails, it's often quite hard to make sense of the situation and getting things moving as they should be.

And apart from the logistical and technical worries, there's also the management of the personalities – if you've engaged a load of individual tradespeople, they may not have worked together before and it's very easy to end up with personality clashes when you've got a load of self-employed people working in the same space at the same time. I've had people walk of jobs because of it and the aggravation plus finding a replacement can really put a dent in your timescale.

So I'd suggest you stand the best chance of getting your project done well and on time if you employ someone to manage it for you. Ask around and get some recommendations for a builder who's got a network of reliable tradespeople. You need a builder anyway, and paying him a little more to be responsible for co-ordinating the work will take a load off your mind and your time. Have a meeting with all the contractors before you start work, make sure everyone's clear about who's in charge and go through the schedule with them all. Then I usually pop along once a week, just to catch up with the project manager and check everything is going to plan.

Get some help from:

- Chapter 4 of my book **'HMO Property Renovation and Refurbishment Success'**, about preparing your team.
- The Nick Fox Property Mentoring office. If you're not sure how to find the right person to employ, we can advise you. Call the office on 01908 930369 or email hello@nickfox.co.uk .

....

"Project managers are the most creative pros in the world; we have to figure out everything that could go wrong, before it does."

Fredrik Haren

Tip 60

Put together a budget and schedule

At each stage of property investment, planning and preparation are key to success. So before you embark on any work, you should put together a budget and a schedule of works. The two overlap, but should be separate documents.

Walk around the property, noting carefully precisely what needs doing in each room and outside. From that, you can allocate a list of jobs and a list of materials required for each job. When you're starting out, it might take you some time to get quotes for everything, but it's worth putting in the effort at this stage. The more accurate your costings, the more reliable your budget will be and you should avoid any nasty surprises.

Involve your builder/project manager, so they can advise on what needs doing and how much it's likely to cost, and don't forget to be very clear on what quotes include, e.g. all labour, all materials and VAT.

Once you have all your costs and quotes, and confirmed jobs, you can put together a schedule for the work. I'd recommend doing this with your project manager – or, at the very least, ask him to check it though for you.

Once you have a clear schedule, share it with the team and have them all confirm they can work to it. The schedule should help keep everyone on track and your budget can be referred to throughout, so you can make sure the actual costs are as you thought they would be. It's a good idea to review these regularly.

Get some help from:

- Chapter 5 of my book **'HMO Property Renovation and Refurbishment Success'** gives much more detailed information on preparing a schedule of works
- MS Excel. The spreadsheet program is perfect for this.

....

"A schedule defends from chaos and whim. It is a net for catching days. It is a scaffolding on which a worker can stand and labor with both hands at sections of time."

Annie Dillard

Tip 61

Don't go cheap

We all know that you get what you pay for, but this knowledge all too often leaves people when they're looking at an expensive project.

The truth is that if you cut costs by too much at the initial renovation & refurbishment stage, you'll have to go back and do much of it again in two or three years, rather than five plus. Things will get tattier and break sooner, and you may even find some items aren't really fit for purpose.

Remember, tenants tend to be harder on a property than owners, and it's especially true if you're doing shorter-term lets or HMOs, where you've got a lot of different people using the fixtures and fittings. Plus cheap usually *looks* cheap and that creates the wrong first impression for prospective tenants.

So think 'cost effective' and head for the middle ground. You don't need to spend a load of money - this isn't your own home – you just need something that's good enough quality to do the job properly. As Phil Spencer says, *"When looking at improving fixtures and fittings — say a £10,000 new kitchen that will boost the rent by only £20 a week — ask yourself if it will increase income or add value to your property. If the answer is neither, it's probably not worth doing."* The reality is that you could probably get a perfectly good, modern kitchen for £4,000 and still be able to charge the same amount of rent as if you'd spent £10,000.

And don't forget that the same applies to paint. Loads of landlords I know go for cheap paint, on the basis that they'll need to repaint regularly, regardless of how much they spend on it. But that's not quite true. If you use a more expensive, harder-wearing paint, you'll find you can clean marks off, rather than having to repaint, and you also need to apply less of it.

It's the same principle for labour – trust me, I've tried it! Cheap workers tend to be unreliable and do rather shoddy work. And when you try to track them down to fix a problem, they're suddenly very elusive. Anyone who has to undercut other tradespeople to get work really can't be very good at their job. So employing a decent, reliable contractor at a fair price is certainly money well spent.

Get some help from:

- Your builder & other tradespeople. They'll have loads of experience of what lasts and what's a waste of money, so take their advice. And if you order supplies though them, they'll often pass on their trade discount – or at least part of it.

"If you think it's expensive to hire a professional to do the job, wait until you hire an amateur."

Red Adair

Tip 62

Five-year proof the property

You've got to outlay a big chunk of capital all at once to get a property ready to rent, so it makes sense to ensure you're not going to need to do any major jobs for at least another 5 years.

At every stage of the renovation, refurbishment and furnishing, think about the life expectancy of everything and if it means spending a little bit more to get a quality or finish that will last, you're better to spend it now. Because I promise you, going back and having to repair or replace things will be a lot more expensive than doing a thorough job in the first place.

For a lot of that, you'll probably need the guidance of your contractors. For example, they might tell you they can simply patch the plaster in a room, but that one wrong knock or nail could mean yet another patch is necessary. That would be disruptive to tenancies and cash flow, so if re-plastering the whole room would give you peace of mind for the foreseeable future, I'd say it's worth spending the extra.

As well as the extent and quality of work required to five-year proof the property, there's the services, electrics and fire systems. Letting regulations are changing all the time, so go over and above what's currently required. Look at having a control panel fire alarm system installed, even if you're only currently required to have smoke alarms. Either include, or make sure you've allowed space for white goods, including a dishwasher and tumble dryer. If tenant requirements change, your property will look a mess if you have to squeeze in these things where they don't necessarily belong.

And make sure there's the facility for superfast fibre broadband. You might not need or want to offer it to your tenants right now, but it's likely to become essential in the very near future.

Get some help from:
- Your team of contractors.
- Letting agents. Ask them what tenants are beginning to ask for and also what they think is likely to change legislation-wise that could affect your property.

....

"Always plan ahead. It wasn't raining when Noah built the ark."

Richard Cardinal Cushing

Tip 63

Have weekly team meetings

Your project manager, assuming you have one, should be keeping your project on track on a daily basis. While neither he nor his team will thank you for hovering over them every day, it's a good idea to agree one day each week when you'll have a meeting at the property.

Go through the schedule with your project manager and ask check that he's happy with how everything's progressing. This gives him a chance to chat through non-urgent queries with you and update you if there are any delays – or if they're ahead of schedule! Walk around the property together so that he can show you the works and you can query anything you're not happy with. It's far easier to put things right as the work's being done, rather than waiting until the end to snag, then finding things need to be undone and redone.

Aside from the actual works, it's good for the morale of the people on site if they see that you're interested and encouraging. Always arrive with some refreshments – chocolate biscuits never fail to please! – and you might want to check with your PM the day before whether there's anything the team particularly like. If you go in the morning, take some bacon and sausage rolls; if you go at lunchtime, arrive with some nice sandwiches.

Before you leave, make sure you've thanked everyone for their hard work and agreed with your project manager any amendments to the schedule for the next week. And take some photos, so you've got a visual record of the work, especially if there's anything you're not happy with, then you can compare improvements and progress on your next visit.

Get some help from:
* nickfox.co.uk

....

Team happiness tip: get together a tray for the property with a kettle, mugs, spoons, tea, coffee, sugar, long-life milk and a Tupperware box of biscuits so as & when they can plug something in, they can make themselves refreshments. And remember to top up supplies when you go for your weekly meetings. You'll be amazed how much sugar contractors can go through!

Tip 64

Hold back 10% until snagging is complete

This is completely normal for a property project, so don't feel awkward bringing it up with your project manager – he'll probably be expecting it.

Obviously, you should make a careful inspection of the property as soon as all the work's finished, and give your project manager immediate feedback. But a lot of what's done will take time to settle down, so you might not see any problems for days or even weeks.

Plaster and paint could crack when dry, so you might need to get it filled. You should go through and check all the electrics, especially things like using a lot of sockets at once, because you can be sure your tenants will have most of them in use most of the time – especially in HMOs. So 'play around' with having the cooker, kettle and room sockets all on the go at once, along with lights in all the rooms, and make sure the circuit can take it.

Check doors all open and close properly, any fire safety features work as they should and that the heating system functions property on full – run a bath, turn on the shower and put all the radiators on high. Note any drops in temperature and listen for any odd noises. And so on.

You should get warranties/guarantees from each of your contractors, but still hold back on paying the final 10% of your works bill until you're sure everything has been done correctly and you're happy with the way it looks and works. I'd suggest delaying payment for 4 weeks, which should be plenty of time for any problems to come to light.

Get some help from:
- Chapter 9 of my book **'HMO Property Renovation and Refurbishment Success'**, about tying up your project.

....

snagging n.
Pronunciation: /ˈsnagɪŋ/
The process of checking a new building for minor faults that need to be rectified.

Tip 65

Don't pay in cash

Some tradespeople will offer you a discount if you pay them in cash, or simply say they'd rather take cash. That might sound appealing, but you shouldn't take them up on it.

The reason most of them are likely to be asking for cash is because they're planning not to run your job through their books. If they're offering you a discount, that's usually because they can knock off the VAT: if they're not declaring it, they're not paying VAT on it!

From your perspective, while you're not doing anything illegal if you pay cash, morally, you shouldn't be facilitating tax evasion. But the practical implications are potentially messy. Unless there is a proper invoice and record of the work that they've done, there's unlikely to be a warranty or guarantee, so if something goes wrong, you might have a job getting it put right without paying.

The other problem is that, because cash payments often don't come with an invoice, you won't be able to claim any of the work as tax-deductible. And your accountant won't like that!

Get some help from:

- The government website, which has information on VAT fraud: gov.uk/report-vat-fraud
- Our office. If you have any queries about whether you should pay someone in cash, we may be able to give you an answer or some advice. Call us on 01908 930369 or email hello@nickfox.co.uk

....

'Fourteen per cent of 2,000 homeowners polled said they would rather pay less money for a service by paying cash, even if they knew the tradesman was avoiding tax. 51 per cent didn't believe there was anything wrong with paying cash-in-hand, meanwhile, 36 per cent of homeowners have specifically asked for a discount in exchange for paying cash.'

Confused.com survey, reported in The Daily Mail, May 2014

Tip 66

Remember it's not your home

Sometimes it's hard to be completely objective when you're getting a property ready to rent, but - at every stage - let your research and your budget guide you.

You might prefer one set of taps, but if another set are half the price, almost as nice-looking and will do the job just as well, go for those. The colour you'd choose for your own walls might not be in the trade range, but just go for the closest thing – the tenants won't mind. In your own home, you might like curtains, but in a lot of rental properties, blinds are more suitable.

If you're furnishing the property, you might gravitate towards a particular colour or style, but look at what other people are providing, ask a good local letting agent for advice and get something fairly neutral, hard-wearing and easy to clean. That's important. You might like pale suede or linen for a sofa, but that's going to get dirty and stained very easily.

The hard-wearing and easy to clean element is especially important if you're furnishing an HMO and you might end up buying furniture you personally actively dislike! So be prepared for that.

Get some help from:

- Other landlords. Pick their brains and ask if you can have a look at their properties. Otherwise, make some appointments with a letting agent to see what kind of accommodation other landlords are providing.

....

"Shelve all your own tastes, likes and dislikes and look at each property from a business point of view. You want a property that performs well in the chosen market, rather than something you want to live in yourself."

Kate Faulkner, Daily Mail, June 2015

Tip 67

Use the same interior scheme for all properties

If you're a creative sort, this might sound a bit dull, but it makes very good business sense, assuming you're looking at buy to let outside the very high-end market.

Firstly, if you're building a portfolio, you're building a business and it's a good idea for your business to have a consistent brand image. Once people realise that all your accommodation is of the same look and quality, they'll be more likely to recommend or commit to renting it, without having necessarily seen the specific property or room that's available. And it makes advertising so much easier if you can use just a few standard photos.

If you're using the same supplies and suppliers time and again, and choosing items from their core ranges, you can often negotiate discounts for buying in bulk and know you'll be able to replace items quickly and easily.

Having the same paint colour throughout every property means you avoid having to store lots of different part-used pots and it'll make refreshing the paintwork so much more straightforward for your handyman or decorator. The same applies to your carpet fitter.

Sticking to one standard scheme also means you'll quickly be able to build a standard budget for the fixtures, fittings, furnishing and décor, and shopping for the items will be as easy as it can be. With every new property acquisition, you'll get better and faster at pulling together an accurate budget.

Get some help from:

- Chapter 8 of my book, **'HMO Renovation and Refurbishment Success'**, which has more detailed information on developing a standard theme
- Furniture package companies, such as davidphillips. com and landlordfurnitureuk.co.uk. If you don't want to have to go out and find furniture yourself, companies like these can offer an all-in-one solution

....

"Simplify your life. Strip away all that is unimportant - then focus, focus, focus. You'll be surprised how good you will then get at being great."

Robin S. Sharma

Tip 68

Use the right paint

I've touched on this in other tips, but here's a whole one on the rather mundane but important subject of paint.

Firstly, no matter how good/hard-wearing/waterproof paint is, if you want to keep the property looking fresh and appealing to tenants, you are going to have to repaint far more often than you would your own home, so don't go for expensive stuff.

Then make sure you choose the right paint for each room:

- For most of the interior walls, choose something neutral from a trade range, which will be durable. You should be able to clean off most marks.
- In kitchens, use specialist paint that's grease and stain resistant
- In bathrooms, use moisture and steam-resistant paint on the walls and anti-mould paint on the ceiling and around windows. If you choose to use standard bathroom paint, make sure you use an anti-mould treatment/spray when you carry out periodical maintenance.
- Use gloss, rather than eggshell on woodwork, as it's harder-wearing.

Get some help from:

- diy.com – B&Q have some good decorating advice and stock a good choice of paints.

....

'While it is a good idea to use a mould resistant paint, getting to the root of the problem should always be your priority. Try to discover why you have mould in your bathroom before you try covering it up.'

Megan Collins Quinlan, for plumbworld.co.uk

Tip 69

Fit an appropriate boiler

The first thing to bear in mind is that not every plumber is experienced in fitting boilers in rental properties, so although you might expect them to know what's right for your property, you can't rely on that.

You've got to consider the weight of use on the boiler. A flat let to one couple who are out at work during the day will need one type and standard of boiler; a 6-bedroom HMO with 6 or more people possibly working different shifts and using sinks, showers, baths and radiators all at the same time, will require a much more resilient – and expensive - type of boiler.

Tenants hate hot water and heating faults more than probably any other issue, so it's really important to make sure the boiler in the property can cope with what's expected of it. Be very clear with your plumber about how much use it's going to get and if they're at all hesitant, get a second opinion.

You also need to make sure the boiler's fitted securely – or rather, that the controls are secure. If tenants are able to get to the valves etc., they have a tendency to fiddle with them and can end up causing problems that can be costly to fix. So I'd recommend asking your carpenter or handyman to box it in when it's fitted.

Get some help from:

- Gassaferegister.co.uk. Only use plumbers who are on the register and legally able to work on gas appliances

....

Extra tip for HMOs: if you fit all electric showers in your property, that will take some of the strain off the boiler. It also means that if the boiler breaks down, the tenants can still have hot showers.

Tip 70

Consider getting 'suited' keys

When I first found out about master suited locks and keys, it was a revelation. If you don't know about them, this is a system that allows you to hold one master key that opens numerous locks, and then issue other keys with limited access. And the levels for each key can be customised. It's really very clever.

That means that you, as a landlord – and/or your property manager – can hold just one key that opens all the locks in all your properties, while a tenant in an HMO could be given a key that only opens their room door, the front door and the back door.

They are more expensive than standard and restricted keys (that can't be duplicated without authorisation) so you need to weigh up the cost against the benefits for yourself.

On the plus side, it's a time saver and a space saver and can be hugely convenient if you're carrying out inspections or showing several rooms in different properties. You can also issue your handyman with just one key that gets him into to all the areas he might need to access.

Get some help from:

- Locksmiths.co.uk, the website for the Master Locksmiths Association, where you can search for a member near you
- Your local landlords association. Ask around and see who's using a master suited key system and what they think of it.

....

"You've got to think about big things while you're doing small things, so that all the small things go in the right direction."

Alvin Toffler

Tip 71

Put a lockable shed in the garden

There are two reasons for this. Firstly, it means there's somewhere for you to store materials and supplies for the property, such as tins of paint or outdoor furniture in the winter. And secondly, it gives your tenants somewhere to store bikes, canoes, tents, etc. that you often otherwise find cluttering up hallways, landings and living rooms.

It's not so much that these things aren't very nice to look at in the house, it's more that every time the tenants wrestle them in and out, walls and doorways get scraped, marked and chipped, and carpets get unnecessarily dirty. So it makes sense for you to offer them some secure outside storage.

Remind your tenants that if they are storing anything outside the property, they're responsible for making sure it's insured. Do fit a good padlock and it's advisable to have a motion-activated light outside that will illuminate the shed, to deter any burglars.

Get some help from:
- Your gardener or handyman – they might know the best place to get hold of good sheds and security for them.

'Garden sheds are a very popular target with burglars and are often overlooked when security is being considered. It is wise to secure the shed door with at least one heavy duty hasp and closed-shackle padlock. In addition, it is worth considering the installation of an alarm:

  ○ *a passive infra-red detector within the shed*

  ○ *a door contact system*

Both systems will operate a sounder if the shed is accessed without the correct de-activation. They are available with battery or mains power supply and can be purchased from your local locksmiths, D-I-Y or discount store.'

Thames Valley Police, Garden Security Advice

Tip 72

Would you be happy to live there?

Although an investment property isn't your home, don't lose sight of the fact that it is *somebody's* home. The majority of tenants these days aren't just 'lodging' somewhere temporarily; they're renting for longer and longer periods of time.

So, make sure that the standard of facilities, décor, safety and security you're offering is good and the property feels like a nice place to live: clean, well-looked after, up to date and safe.

I've heard of investors who use their children as a barometer, particularly for HMOs: "Would I want my son/daughter to live here?", and that's not a bad way to approach the refurbishment and furnishing of an investment. Would you let your nearest and dearest live in the home you're providing - without any concerns?

Get some help from:
- Friends and family. Ask them what they think – particularly if they've got children who are young adults, and ask the young ones themselves. You have to keep researching your audience and consider the feedback you get.

"We know that when people are safe in their homes, they are free to pursue their dream for a brighter economic future for themselves and their families."

George Pataki

Tip 73

Use an all-in-one utility provider

All-in-one utility providers do exactly what they say: they supply your energy, water, phone, etc. so you only have one company to deal with and one bill coming to you each month.

There's an increasing number of providers out there, so you might want to shop around and take some recommendations, but I think it's well worth using this kind of service. There are some that specialise in shared housing and will even include the TV licence as part of the package, so all you have to worry about on top is the council tax.

Choosing the right provider can make your life and your tenants lives so much easier, as there's only one port of call if there are any problems and, because they have your business across a range of utilities, and every account is therefore relatively important to them, they're motivated to keep you happy and provide a good service.

Having a single bill every month cuts down hugely on admin - multiple bills for every property is a time and money overhead you should avoid if you can. And I've found that having everything under one umbrella is cheaper than having separate providers, plus, when you periodically shop around for better deals, as you should, you're cutting your workload down by at least 75%.

Get some help from:

- Nick Fox Property Mentoring. If you'd like to discuss our provider or have any other queries, call the office on 01908 930369 or email hello@nickfox.co.uk .
- Utilitywarehouse.co.uk. One of the biggest all-in-one providers that a lot of landlords use – have a look at their website to find out more.

....

"Simplicity is the ultimate sophistication."
Leonardo da Vinci

Tip 74

Put together a property file

Whether your tenants end up using/referring to it or not, it's a good idea to put together an information file for each of your rental properties – a bit like you find in holiday cottages!

Letting regulations stipulate that you need to issue your tenants with instructions for the safe use of gas appliances and equipment that you've provided, so they're one thing that certainly needs to go in the file. In addition, it's a good idea to leave instructions for the cooker, washing machine, tumble dryer, fridge freezer, television, etc. If you have any warranties or guarantees, include copies of those as well. Also leave instructions for where to find the stopcock and isolator switches, etc.

Some of the following applies to HMOs only, so pick and choose which things are relevant if you only have single household lets.

Include contact details for whoever's managing the property, along with their 'working hours'. You should also note down details of who to call in an emergency – primarily your electrician and plumber. And if there's broadband to the property, have the router set-up and password details written down.

You also might want to include:

- copies of the gas safety and electrical installation certificates
- a copy of the EPC
- a copy of the prescribed information on the deposit protection scheme you're using
- a copy of the government's 'How to rent' guide that needs to be issued to each new tenant
- a household waste and recycling collection calendar
- key local bus routes
- local taxi firm numbers

Essentially, think about what handy information you have in your admin drawer, stuck on the back of the door or the fridge, etc. and use that as a guide for what to put in the file. Then don't forget to tell the tenants it's there!

Get some help from:

- Friends who have rented – and your own experiences. What did they think it would have been useful to know about?

....

Extra tip: *The government's 'How to rent' guide is frequently updated, so make sure you always use the latest version from the GOV.UK website.*

Tip 75

Insure yourself properly

Insurance for buy to let is different to property insurance for your own home. You need to obtain it from a specialist provider and make sure you've talked though your needs with a professional advisor.

If you're carrying out works after completion, you'll need to be properly insured while the work's going on, then amend it when the property is finished but untenanted, and again when it's occupied.

In addition to buildings insurance, as a landlord, you have a responsibility for the safety of tenants and contractors, so you need public liability insurance that covers you if someone is injured in your property and pursues you for damages.

You should also take out malicious damage insurance, in case one of your tenants deliberately damages the building or the furnishings.

Other cover you should look into and consider includes:
- Flood insurance
- Insurance that covers the cost of alternative accommodation if you have to temporarily re-house your tenants
- Rent guarantee insurance

HMOs require specialist insurance and most of the main landlord insurance providers – including Direct Line – don't deal with them. Although it might not be straightforward to get the cover you need, you must always be completely honest about the tenancy status of the property you're looking to insure, or your cover might be invalid.

Get some help from:
- Your mortgage broker – they should be able to recommend appropriate insurers to approach

....

'Public liability insurance protects you and your buy to let property against claims made by tenants for personal injury or damage to their possessions arising from incidents connected with your property. If the tenant makes a claim against you, and you're found to be legally liable, Public Liability Insurance will cover you for:
- *Damages awarded to the claimant*
- *Your legal costs in defending a claim*
- *The claimant's legal costs, if you're at fault'*

Direct Line for Business

Tip 76

Take photos before any tenants move in!

Your property is never going to look as good again as it does when you've jst finished your refurbishment. Once tenants have moved in, they start taking a toll on all your hard work, so you need to capture it at its best before you let it.

Take some photographs of it as you're going to let it, then focus on taking some really good advertising photos.

Choose a nice day so the property's light inside and looking good on the outside, and dress the rooms so that they look as appealing and inviting as possible.

Make up the bed in the bedroom/s you're photographing, put some lamps on the bedside tables and have a plant or some flowers to add a splash of colour. In the kitchen, stack some cook books on the worktop, put out a bowl of fruit and some nice cooking oils… this might all sound contrived and highly unoriginal, but the truth is, the more generic, the better, because you'll appeal to a broad range of people.

In the living room, have some candles, cushions and throws, a plant or some flowers, and make sure there's a picture or two on the wall – a classic arty black and white print is perfect.

Once you've taken your photos, remember to take all your dressing items away with you. You might be tempted to leave them for the tenants, but if you do, vases will get broken, plants will be left to die…and so on. Because rented properties are often shared spaces, there can be very little sense of responsibility for the communal areas. So leave the rooms in the property as your tenants will want them: clean, functional and easy to keep that way.

Get some help from:
- Property advertising websites, like Rightmove and Spareroom. Look at what kind of photos other landlords are using, take those as a guide - and make yours better!

....

"You never get a second chance to make a first impression."

Will Rogers

Further reading...

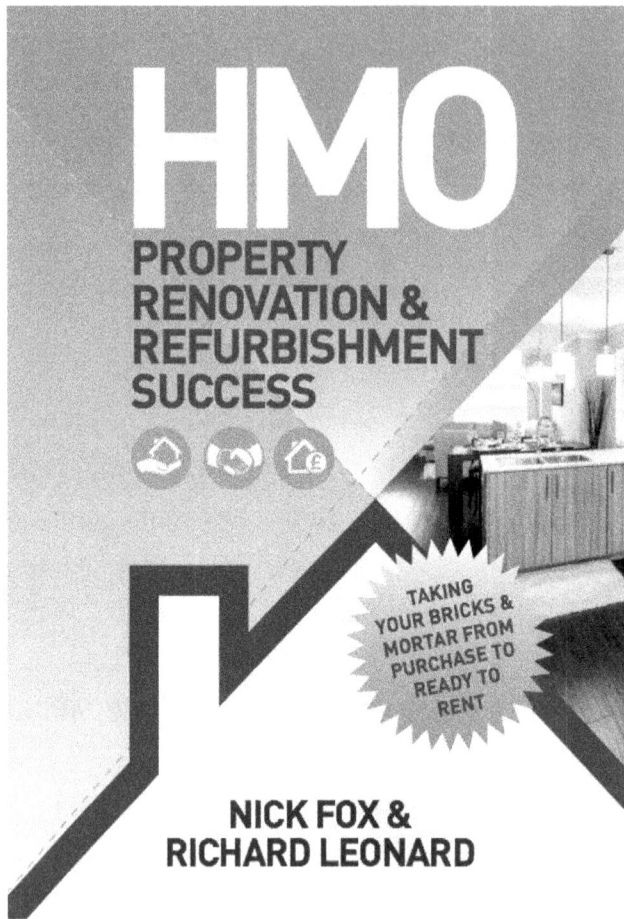

HMO
PROPERTY
RENOVATION &
REFURBISHMENT
SUCCESS

TAKING
YOUR BRICKS &
MORTAR FROM
PURCHASE TO
READY TO
RENT

NICK FOX &
RICHARD LEONARD

For detailed information and advice, and lots more tips on successfully renovating and refurbishing buy to let property, read the book I co-authored with specialist project manager, Richard Leonard.

Available now from:

amazon.co.uk and **nickfox.co.uk**

LETTING & MANAGING

Tip 77

Get yourself accredited

With various licensing and registration schemes for landlords and their properties now in force in Scotland, Wales, Northern Ireland and the City of Liverpool, plus voluntary schemes, such as the London Rental Standard, legislation for the whole of England can't be too far away. In the meantime, while many people are still sceptical about landlords and the standard of accommodation on offer, it's a good idea to get yourself accredited in some way.

If you can demonstrate that you're keen to operate your property investment business in a professional way and have taken advantage of all the training and checks available to you, that should reassure tenants that you're a reputable landlord and should stand you in good stead if you become involved in any legal disputes over your conduct or property. Being part of a professional scheme or associations should also be helpful in keeping up to date with legislation.

Many local authorities offer landlord accreditation schemes, so, although some of these don't seem to be very tightly monitored, it's worth making enquiries in your area. If you're operating HMOs, even if you don't need a licence, the council will still have a register that you must make sure you're on. They will carry out periodical health and safety checks on your properties and issue a letter to confirm whether everything is satisfactory. Make sure you keep your own record of these in case the quality of your properties is challenged.

The National Federation of Property Professionals (NFoPP) awarding body also offers a variety of qualifications. They're aimed at agents, but some are available to private landlords, so if you're planning on making property investment a real business for yourself, it's worth looking into these.

Get some help from:

- Your local council housing department will have information on any accreditation schemes they offer
- Join the National Landlords Association (landlords. org.uk) or the Residential Landlords Association (rla. org.uk) to benefit from support and advice, and as a first step to accreditation
- See what qualifications NFoPP offers, at nfopp-awardingbody.co.uk
- London.gov.uk has details of what you need to do to become recognised under the London Rental Standard

....

"This bold initiative is designed to raise professional standards in the capital's private rented sector by providing a consistent benchmark of accreditation for

consumers. We have long campaigned for regulation of the private rented sector, and it is crucial we eliminate the small minority of unscrupulous landlords and agents who neglect their responsibilities and bring our industry into disrepute. We are proud to be working with the Mayor on this first step towards a more regulated industry."

David Cox, ARLA managing director, on the London Rental Standard, April 2015

Tip 78

Choose a managing agent with the right experience

In the same way as you're likely to have chosen your legal representation, financial advisors and tradespeople based on their relevant experience and expertise in your type of property investment, the same should go for any letting and managing agent you work with.

Go through a few pages of lettings listings online, searching for the type of property you're looking to let, and you'll see which agents come up the most. Some – usually the higher-end, larger agents, such as Knight Frank – primarily deal with more expensive family homes, while others will specialise in city-centre apartments, for example. You'll probably end up with a list of 4 or 5 in your area that are worth speaking to.

HMOs are a very specific sector of the market and most agents don't handle room lets, which is partly why many landlords choose to set up their own lettings and management system. If you're planning on letting to students, contact the university or college accommodation office for advice on which agents tend to deal well with them.

While you were carrying out your initial property research, you should have been speaking to local agents anyway, so will probably have an idea of which one you'd like to use yourself. Ask about their occupancy rates, percentage of tenants in arrears and number of evictions they've had in the last year. Then ask if you can speak to one or two of their current portfolio landlords and do a bit of asking around to see what other landlords generally think of them.

If you can use an agent that has a dedicated buy to let arm to their business, such as Belvoir and Savills, they're likely to be able to give you some very helpful ongoing advice, because they really understand yields and that you're driven by returns. They may offer periodical portfolio reviews, to help you make sure your properties are always doing as well as they can for you.

Get some help from:

*   Propertychecklists.co.uk. Independent property expert and market analyst, Kate Faulkner, has some useful articles and checklists on what to think through when choosing an agent

....

Extra tip: Make sure that whichever agent you choose, they're a member of ARLA, NLA or NALS. That means they adhere to a code of conduct over and above that of The Property Ombudsman and the staff have undergone appropriate training and are up to date with the latest lettings legislation.

Tip 79

Delegate

This is something that you might find hard to do if you're used to keeping a lot of balls in the air, have gained quite a bit of knowledge about the industry and are generally competent. So if you're currently doing pretty much everything yourself – admin, research, project management, shopping, marketing, viewings, check ins, ongoing management, maintenance jobs, bookkeeping, etc. – that's not an unusual.

But it's rarely a good idea. Generally speaking, people who get into property investment as a sideline wealth creation tool, tend to be quite driven and therefore capable of earning good money. So cluttering up your valuable time with jobs that could be carried out by someone else is really not good for business.

Added to that is the fact that it's virtually impossible to excel at everything and most of the tasks involved in running a property portfolio are best handed over to someone who's dedicated to that one task.

If you employ an agent or private property manager and a bookkeeper as a minimum, that'll free you up from most of the admin and time-consuming tasks that don't, strictly speaking, earn you money. Then you can focus on making your current investments as profitable as possible, new acquisitions and other property projects.

Or, quite simply, you can take a bit more time to yourself. Remember, you're in this to ultimately improve your quality of life and standard of living, so make sure you're not filling every day with jobs you're over-qualified for.

And if you're worried about the cost impact of paying other people, I can honestly say that every employee, advisor and contractor I pay and every service I take advantage of, ultimately makes me more profitable.

Get some help from:

- Books on the subject. 'Delegate to Elevate: 7 Steps to Success for Sole Traders' by Sally Marshall, for example, has some very helpful content

....

"Surround yourself with the best people you can find, delegate authority, and don't interfere as long as the policy you've decided upon is being carried out."

Ronald Reagan

Tip 80

Reference your tenants properly

It's not only sensible to check your tenants' identity, credit history, employment status and whether they can afford their rent, some aspects are required.

It's not uncommon for lender to stipulate in the terms of your buy to let mortgage agreement that any tenant on an AST must be referenced via an appropriate credit check company, and it may also be a condition of your insurance.

And, from 1st February 2016, every prospective tenant has to undergo Right to Rent checks, meaning you or your managing agent have to obtain proof that the tenant has the legal right to be in the UK.

So set up some referencing procedures for every new tenant that applies to rent from you. If you use an agent, they should be carrying this out on your behalf – it's worth finding out exactly what checks they perform – but if you're handling it yourself, I'd suggest you do the following:

- Ask to see their original passport or other identity papers that prove their right to be in the country
- Request their last 3 months' bank statements so you

can see their income and expenditure patterns
- Take a reference from their employer and/or previous landlord
- Carry out a credit check via the NLA, Experian or another suitable agent
- Take a note of their registration number if they have a car

Nine times out of ten, if a tenant is dodgy, they're likely to try and wriggle out of some of these, so only proceed with those who are happy to be entirely open with you.

Get some help from:
- Nlatenantcheck.org. If you're a member of the NLA, you save £5 on every check
- The GOV.UK site, which has all the information you need about Right to Rent checks, including the Home Office checking service for cases where a tenant's immigration status is unclear.

....

Extra tip: *Some tenants have been known to use friends to give references. Make sure work references are valid by ringing the main company switchboard, rather than a direct dial, so you know you're speaking to the person you think you are!*

Tip 81

Get an independent inventory

I've come across some terrible inventories in my time, carried out by landlords who think just listing what's included in their property, along with a casual 'good' or 'used' scribbled next to each item, is all they need to do. While that would have been considered poor ten years ago, a lot of landlords weren't that bothered because if they felt tenants had caused any damage, etc., they'd just keep hold of a large chunk of the deposit – if not all of it.

But since deposit protection laws came into force in 2007, it's been in your own best interest to have a professional inventory taken, given that tenants can challenge any amount you want to retain and you'll need to be able to prove beyond doubt that theft or damage occurred during the tenancy and not before or after. That means a clear record, signed and dated by the tenant, that they can't dispute, and if it's been carried out by an independent inventory clerk, you've got a 3rd party, unbiased witness.

A good inventory should record the content and condition of every room in detail - the ceiling, walls, floor/carpet, fixtures and fittings and all the contents - with photographs that back up what's written down. Far from the 'couple of sheets' that you'd often see in the old days, these days the inventory on even a one-bedroom flat can easily run to 20 pages.

If you're using a letting agent, most will offer an inventory service, but if you're choosing one yourself, make sure they're a member of the Association of Independent Inventory Clerks (AIIC). That means you can be confident they'll have professional indemnity and public liability insurance, abide by a professional code of conduct and will be properly trained. Clerks may offer additional services, including periodical inspections and full check ins and outs.

Get some help from:

- Theaiic.co.uk, where you can search for an independent clerk in your area
- No Letting Go, which is an excellent inventory service franchise – nolettinggo.co.uk

"Over 90% of cases through the MyDeposits deposit scheme award against landlords – a lack of inventory at the check-in stage is a major reason for this."

nolettinggo.co.uk, December 2015

Tip 82

Keep on top of maintenance

You might be able to overlook and put off little maintenance jobs in your own home, but in order to attract and keep the best tenants, paying a good level of rent, you mustn't give them any reason to not want to pay what you're asking. It's just like when you're selling your home: do all you can to make the property look worth every penny.

You might sometimes feel as though you're always paying little maintenance bills, but I can assure you, it's much better to pay out small amounts more often than wait for something to break or wear out. Not only is that usually more expensive to put right, your tenants won't appreciate the inevitable delay and inconvenience while whatever it is gets fixed.

So schedule regular maintenance checks – I'd suggest once every 4 months – and ask your contractors to let you know if there's anything else they think needs refreshing while they're there. Some landlords I know give their handyman carte blanche to just go ahead with any little jobs under £50. Show your tenants you're proactive about maintenance.

From a legal and health & safety point of view, you must make sure your gas and electrical systems and equipment are checked when they should be and the correct certification obtained. If you don't organise gas safety, domestic electrical installation and portable appliance checks according to regulations and something happens that causes damage to your property or injures tenants, not only could your insurance be declared invalid, but you might face fines and even prison.

And don't forget to carry out an annual 'wind and water-tight' check before the bad winter weather sets in. Clear out gutters and drains, make sure no roof tiles are missing or damaged, look for any missing pointing or cracks in brickwork, check seals on doors and windows and ensure any external pipework. It's also a good idea to double-check your insurance policy, to make sure you've done everything they stipulate to keep your cover valid.

Get some help from:

- Propertychecklists.co.uk, which has useful free maintenance-related checklists and some helpful articles on good practice and regulations.

....

"You must get good at one of two things. Planting in the spring or begging in the fall."

Jim Rohn

Tip 83

Respond to tenants quickly

This really is common sense. If someone has a problem or a complaint, the first thing they're looking for is to have it acknowledged. You might think their complaint is non-urgent or even petty, but it's important enough for them to have contacted you. And remember, very few people really enjoy complaining! So get back to them as quickly as possible to find out exactly what's wrong and what they expect you to do, then address and resolve it.

That's always been considered good practice, but now it's also in your best interests. On 1st October 2015, new rules came into force preventing landlords from 'retaliatory' or 'revenge' evictions. That's where a landlord used to be able to issue a section 21 notice to a tenant simply because they were fed up with them complaining, then would evict them if they didn't leave.

You can't do that any more. If a tenant can prove that they had a legitimate complaint about the property's condition, which they put to you in writing, and you failed to respond and make proper repairs, any section 21 you served after they complained can be declared invalid by the council. And that could make getting rid of what you see as a 'problem' tenant very tricky.

So make sure you've got a reliable team of contractors that you know will attend to jobs quickly for you and that you document everything you do and say following a tenant's complaint or any report that something's wrong with the property. As long as you can show you're doing all you can, you shouldn't encounter any problems.

Get some help from:

- The Shelter website – england.shelter.org.uk. In the 'Get advice' section, there's a lot of information about a landlord's obligation to make repairs and revenge evictions. It's often very useful to see things like this from a tenant's perspective and find out what advice they're being given.

....

"Complaining not only ruins everybody else's day, it ruins the complainer's day too. The more we complain, the more unhappy we get."

Dennis Prager

Tip 84

Record everything – in writing and photos

This should start before your first tenant checks in and be ongoing. There's nothing worse than knowing something was said or done by someone and not being able to prove it when push comes to shove.

So have a proper professional inventory carried out before a tenant moves in and make sure they sign it. When periodical inspections are carried out, make sure photos are taken there and then of any damage and preferably signed off by the tenant. You need to ensure there can be no disputing what they're responsible for paying for when their tenancy ends.

Carefully record all complaints: who made them and when; what action was taken and when; the outcome and confirmation that the tenant was satisfied. If you have any phone conversations with the tenant, make sure you follow it up in an email or letter, to confirm what was said and what further action needs to be taken, if necessary.

If a tenant falls behind with their rent, be sure to act right away and keep a careful paper trail of any repayment terms you've offered and they've agreed.

When fire alarms are tested, gas and electrical safety checks carried out and meters read, etc,, take photographs of the condition of the equipment and any relevant readings. I have a very handy app on my tablet that I've used for inventories, where you can log maintenance, type reports and take photos, then email the whole thing, which will date and time stamp it.

At some point you're like to have to begin eviction proceedings against a tenant or pursue them legally for some reason, and you'll be much better placed to have the matter resolved as quickly as possible if you've got clear evidence.

Get some help from:

- An independent inventory clerk, who can handle check ins, periodical inspections and check outs, and make professional reports. Find one near you via theaiic. co.uk

A picture is worth a thousand words.

Tip 85

Review your finances every 6 months

I actually look at my income and expenditure more often than that, but every 6 months is probably sufficient.

It's surprising how much your profits can be increased by making even small changes to your costs and rental income. Speak to your mortgage broker to see if it's worth switching products or lenders and look at whether you could remortgage and release capital to reinvest into another property.

Contact utility providers to find out if you could save money by moving. If you use an all-in-one provider, this shouldn't take very long and if you currently have all your utilities with different companies, I'd highly recommend you looking into putting them all under one umbrella, which should save you time and money.

Compare your yield with the market average and check you're keeping ahead of that, and make sure your return on investment figure is better than you could be getting elsewhere.

Then look at your rent and see whether you could be putting it up. Make sure you do some solid research before doing that, as you don't want to upset good tenants. Remember, it's voids that kill!

But look at how much your rents have gone up across the board over the last 3 years. Taking inflation at an average of 3% a year, if your rents haven't been climbing by at least that much each year, bear in mind the value of your income is essentially going down.

Even if you don't want to necessarily change anything about your current income and expenditure, it's still good practice to analyse your financial position regularly. You should always know more or less what your KPIs are and whether your investments are beating market averages.

Get some help from:

- The viability analysis spreadsheet template that you can find in the 'Downloadable Templates' section of my website at **nickfox.co.uk**. It breaks down all your income and expenditure and helps you calculate your KPIs
- Your financial advisors. They'll be able to recommend any changes you could make that would increase your profits.

....

'Cheaper and better rates and deals come onto the market all the time. If you don't review your savings and investments regularly you stand to lose money. In fact, many banks, building societies and product providers rely on you doing nothing! Set a regular review date, at

least once a year, that allows enough time to make the most of your tax allowances – go for at least two months before the end of the tax year.'

moneyadviceservice.org.uk

Tip 86

Don't push your rent too high

Just because your costs have risen, inflation has been at a higher rate than your rent increases or you've refurbished and feel you 'deserve' more rent, that doesn't mean you can or should put it up.

If you currently have a tenant who pays their rent on time, seems to be treating the property well and currently has no plans to leave, you have to weigh up whether it's reasonable to ask for a small increase in rent with the danger that they might leave, especially if there's a good choice of alternative accommodation. If your property is of a good standard and you're already getting a relatively high rent, it may be more sensible not to risk a void. Would the gain be worth risking the potential loss of income?

If you don't currently have a tenant, 'testing the market' at an optimistic rent will probably result in your property sitting empty for a while.

Remember that rents can only go up if people can afford to pay more, so you need to look at the local economy and find out whether things are on the up and wages are rising. Rent rises also depend on whether tenants *have* to pay more, so you must check supply and demand. If there's a lot of choice out there, it's not the right time to be a bit cheeky.

Get some help from:
- Lslps.co.uk, which issues a monthly buy to let index, with analysis and commentary, including data on arrears
- Ons.gov.uk, which releases a quarterly index on the PRS

....

When your landlord can increase rent
For a periodic tenancy, your landlord can't normally increase the rent more than once a year without your agreement.
For a fixed-term tenancy, your landlord can only increase the rent if you agree. If you don't agree, the rent can only be increased when the fixed term ends.
For any tenancy:
- *your landlord must get your permission if they want to increase the rent by more than previously agreed*
- *the rent increase must be fair and realistic, ie in line with average local rents*

gov.uk/private-renting/rent-increases

Tip 87

Do all you can to keep voids to a minimum

Depending on how great your cash flow is, a void could wipe out a good portion of your annual profit; in the worst case, all of it. And while you're not getting any income, you still have mortgage repayments and maintenance bills to cover.

I've met a lot of landlords who turn down tenants that offer slightly below the advertised rent because they feel it's worth what they're asking – it's a fair market rent. And they don't do the maths. Say you're asking £500 a month and someone offers you £475. Over a six-month tenancy period, that amounts to a 'loss' of £150. If your property sits empty for two weeks, you've lost more than that right away. If the market's strong and you or your letting agent is rightly confident that another tenant will sign up to the full asking rent within days, then fair enough, but if things are a bit slow, it might be a mistake to reject the offer.

On top of not currently producing any income, an untenanted property can begin to feel cold and unloved. You've got to air it regularly and if the weather's damp, check that condensation and surface mould aren't forming. If it's a cold time of year, you'll also have to pay to have the heating on, plus you've got to make sure mail's not piling up. The longer your void, the more likely it is you'll have to reduce your asking rent.

So do what you can to keep hold of good tenants, advertise early when you know current tenants are leaving and make sure your property is well maintained and appealing, so that you attract the tenants that are out there.

Get some help from:
- Online rental portals. Advertised rents are usually fairly accurate, so keep an eye on local rents to make sure you're not overcharging and putting tenants off.

....

"Your life is an occasion. Rise to it."

Suzanne Weyn

Tip 88

Act quickly if tenants are late paying

If rent doesn't come in on time and in full, it affects your cash flow – plus it's irritating having to chase up tenants and keep checking your bank account to see whether anything's gone in. But, more importantly, it can be a sign that things are about to 'head south' with your tenant.

So contact the tenant right away – the day after rent was due – to find out why it hasn't been received. There could be a simple explanation, such as they'd forgotten to make the payment, a standing order form hadn't been processed in time with the bank, or their employer hadn't paid their wages on time. On the other hand, it could be more serious. They might be 'short' this month and cagey about when they'll be able to pay you, or they might avoid you completely because they have no intention of paying at all.

If there's a good explanation, then ask them to confirm when the payment will be made and stay on top of it. If things look more suspicious, try to have an honest conversation with the tenant and see whether you can come to an agreement for them to leave the property early. If it gets nasty, you might have to serve notice for them to leave and be prepared to evict them.

The key is to act quickly at every stage, because every day you're not receiving rent, your profits are affected. Be fair and reasonable with your tenant, but make sure you don't make decisions simply because you feel sorry for them. My experience is that once a tenant gets behind with their rent, they're rarely able to make it up. You can offer to help them look for alternative accommodation, but if they can't or won't pay your rent, you need to get them out as soon as possible, so that you can get a paying tenant in.

Make sure everything's confirmed in writing, at every stage, and take specialist advice about serving notices and beginning eviction proceedings.

Get some help from:
- Your letting agent. Even if they're not collecting the rent, they should be happy to advise you.
- Specialist eviction companies, such as Landlord Action (landlordaction.co.uk)
- Landlord Law (landlordlaw.co.uk), which provides legal advice and support for landlords

....

'Tenant arrears in England are up and represented 9.9% of all rent payable in August. While many people have seen their incomes rise and landlords have been able to raise rents accordingly, others have not yet received a

wage boost and it appears to be these people who are finding it hard to make their monthly payments.'

Reeds Rains landlord newsletter, October 2015

Tip 89

Use a legal eviction specialist

Even if you do everything in your power to avoid getting to this point, I should warn you that it's highly likely you'll need to evict a tenant at some point.

While it is certainly possible to handle the eviction process yourself, you shouldn't even begin to tackle it unless you've taken specialist legal advice. Even then, if you don't follow the correct procedure to the letter, you run the risk of a court deeming it an unlawful eviction and you may have to start the whole process from scratch. That increases your legal costs and delays getting a troublesome and/or non-paying tenant out of your property.

I'd suggest it's far less stressful and more effective to pay for the services of an eviction specialist. To be honest, it's not much more expensive than trying to do it yourself and a professional will get things done in a fraction of the time you could - and probably with greater success.

If you do decide to tackle it yourself, are successful and a court grants you possession, bear in mind that if the tenant refuses to move out by the court-appointed date, you'll have to employ a bailiff to eject them from the property. That's the one part of the process you **cannot** legally do yourself.

Get some help from:

- Specialist eviction companies, such as Landlord Action (landlordaction.co.uk)
- Landlord Law (landlordlaw.co.uk), which provides legal advice and support for landlords

....

'The number of tenants evicted from their homes is at a six-year high. County court bailiffs in England and Wales evicted more than 11,000 families in the first three months of 2015, an increase of 8% on the same period last year and 51% higher than five years ago.'

The Guardian, May 2015

Tip 90

Know when to let it go!

When a tenant leaves owing you money, you naturally want to pursue them for it – it's yours and they've got to pay you! But you need to take a step back and consider whether it's actually worth going after the debt.

Do you know exactly where they are and that they can definitely afford to pay you? Even if you did manage to take them to court, a court can't order them to pay with money they don't have. You could spend time and money chasing them for nothing – and it does take a toll on you.

There is another option, which is cheaper than going through the courts, and that's to use the government's Money Claim Online process, which you can do if the debt is less than £100,000. Your legal advisor should be able to help you decide which route to go down.

The third option is simply to let it go and that's the one I usually choose. If you've been efficient and effective at dealing with non-payment of rent, successfully evicted the tenant and re-let the accommodation in as short a period of time as possible, then just write off the debt and move on.

Get some help from:

- Money Claim Online: GOV.UK/make-money-claim-online

....

"The secret of change is to focus all of your energy, not on fighting the old, but on building the new."

Socrates

Tip 91

Develop systems

What I mean by this is if you can work out a process and put the cogs into the machine that executes the process, that machine should be able to turn over without you. And that's what you should always be aiming for, as a businessperson and an investor: to have as passive an investment as possible that generates a return without you having to trade your time for money.

If I stopped doing what I do tomorrow, my portfolio would continue to tick over and make money. It wouldn't necessarily generate the highest possible returns and it wouldn't necessarily grow, but because I've got systems that work and people that I pay to operate them for me, I've built an investment business that gives me an almost 100% passive income.

I say 'almost', because I do need to spend a little time managing and consulting with my team, but for the most part I'm surplus to requirements on a day-to-day basis!

So work out what you want to achieve, spend a few years learning how to achieve it, then employ good people to follow your systems. It's as 'simple' as that...

Get some help from:

- Me and my team. Contact us at the office to discuss how our mentoring programmes could help you build a successful property investment business model: call 01908 930369 or email hello@nickfox.co.uk
- 'Process to Profit', by Marianne Page – available on Amazon.co.uk

....

Systems and time management are the best-kept secrets of the wealthy!

Tip 92

Pay contractors quickly

Having a team of contractors you can rely on to help you out with maintenance issues on an ongoing basis is pretty essential to successful property management. So how do you get them to prioritise your work?

Having a good relationship helps and telling them how pleased you are with what they've done and how much you appreciate their work also puts some brownie points in the bank. But what really makes the difference is if you always pay them quickly.

You know yourself how important cash flow is to your property business, and it's just as important for contractors, especially self-employed ones. Plenty of people and companies they deal with will delay payment of their invoices until the next accounts 'run', so if you can make payment within a couple of days, they'll really appreciate it. And if they can rely on you paying them for their work as soon as they've done it, they'll be keen to do more jobs for you. It's a win/win: you get the job done, they get their money.

On the flip side, if you get a reputation as someone who always needs to be chased more than once for payment, people will be reluctant to do work for you. At the very least, they won't hurry to help you out when your tenants are complaining, and that will become a problem for you.

So be fair: when someone's done a good job, settle your bill.

Get some help from:

- Your local landlords association or networking events. Find out what other landlords consider a reasonable timescale to pay local contractors, then you can either keep in line or beat them!

....

3. Payment - obligations
Your right to be paid
You can set your own payment terms, such as discounts for early payment and payment upfront.
*Unless you agree a payment date, the customer must pay you **within 30 days** of getting your invoice or the goods or service.*

gov.uk

ONWARDS & UPWARDS

Tip 93

Refer and recommend

A lot of success in the property investment industry is down to recommendations and referrals. People who are reliable, good at what they do, and pleasant and easy to deal with are rarely short of work.

You could call it karma: if you do someone a favour by recommending their services or referring them to someone who can help them, then they'll return that favour at some point. When you take time to build a relationship with contractors and pay them on time, they're likely to tell other contractors that you're great to work for. And then, when you refer them to another landlord and they do a good job, that landlord will be more likely to help you out with referrals when you need a particular service or professional.

Essentially, when someone's done a good job or given you particularly helpful advice, or a great lead, it's the right thing to do to spread the word that they're reliable, helpful and decent. That's how you build a network of good people who can continue to boost you and your business.

Get some help from:

- Local business and property networking events. Take the time to introduce yourself to people and find out about them. By the time you've been to two or three, you'll find the same names keep coming up…

....

"Successful people are always looking for opportunities to help others. Unsuccessful people are always asking, "What's in it for me?"

Brian Tracy

Tip 94

Spread your risk

If you've done your homework, you shouldn't be taking too many risks, but what I'm suggesting here is that you don't put all your investment eggs in one basket.

Property is a brilliantly flexible asset class and there are a whole host of things you can invest in, including:

- Residential buy to let – family homes, single lets, multi lets, corporate lets, commercial, etc.
- Commercial leasing
- Development
- Self build
- Land
- Holiday lets
- And more…

…and if you can buy property that has the potential to go down more than one investment route, so much the better. You never know when things might change in certain sectors of the market – already the Government is targeting the tax benefits of buy to let. So it's sensible to give yourself options and ensure your ongoing financial security isn't solely reliant on one type of tenant demand, for example.

You can also limit your risk by investing in joint ventures and taking on partners, and also vary the type of risk you take. Perhaps invest some of your capital into lower-risk single let properties and then periodically do a higher-risk development deal, which will bring you a different type of return.

Get some help from:

- My book, '**Property Investment Success**', which looks at the different ways of making money from property

....

"Life is more risk management, rather than exclusion of risks."

Walter Wriston

Tip 95

Take regular tax advice

Your property tax advisor has a big part to play in how much of the wealth you create you manage to keep hold of.

You should consult them on what you buy, when you buy it, how you buy it, and how you take income or capital returns from it. They can then help you minimise how much of it you pay tax on and delay payment of that tax where possible. So if there's one advisor you should meet with regularly, it's this one.

There are a lot of property-specific tax laws, that's why it's important that whoever is giving you tax advice is familiar with the finer details of property tax and preferably an investor themselves.

If you're thinking of disposing of any assets, talk to your tax advisor before you do anything. They may advise you to split the sales between tax years so you can take full advantage of your personal capital gains allowance. They might recommend you buy, hold and sell property through a company. As your portfolio grows, it may be beneficial for your spouse or a business partner to own or take income from a property, to take advantage of lower tax rate…the list goes on.

Another big thing to appreciate is that Capital Gains Tax is payable on the increase in a property's value from the original purchase price – it's got nothing to do with the equity you walk away with when you sell. So if you're remortgaging, communicate with your tax advisor to make sure they're keeping an eye on your equity levels versus your eventual CGT bill. You don't want to end up owing more to the tax man than you realise from an eventual sale.

The most important thing to remember is that tax rules and regulations change – as we've seen in 2015 – and talking specialist tax advice could make the difference between your portfolio continuing to be profitable and having to exit the industry.

Get some help from:

* tax.org.uk – you can search the Chartered Institute of Taxation database to find a member in your area.

....

"Thinking is one thing no one has ever been able to tax."
Charles Kettering

Tip 96

Aim to retain 25% equity

There are a couple of reasons for this.

Firstly, given that most reasonable buy to let mortgage rates kick in at 75%, you're going to need a minimum 25% equity if you want to remortgage. Otherwise, you may find yourself trapped with a product that's not doing you any favours.

And secondly, having a buffer of that size means that if capital values were to fall again, you'd be insulated – they're highly unlikely to drop by a quarter. Many of the landlords who got into serious trouble did so because they'd leveraged highly and when values fell, they quickly found themselves in negative equity. And in buy to let, you never want to find yourself in the position of having to sell when you might not want to.

It's also comforting to know that if you needed to access money for some reason – you never know when your personal circumstances might change – you can drop your asking price a little for a quick sale and still walk away with a decent chunk of capital in your hand.

Get some help from:

- Your financial advisor. They can talk through the benefits and risks of leverage and advise you based on your own personal circumstances

....

"I'm an optimist, but I'm an optimist who carries a raincoat."

Harold Wilson

Tip 97

Keep your Will updated

Often, people are so busy building their portfolio that they forget to set aside time to put their affairs in order with regard to these acquisitions. They're so consumed with buying, refurbishing, letting, networking, checking the tax implications of what they're doing and enjoying building a new business, that the practicalities of what would happen if they suddenly weren't here any more gets either forgotten or sidelined.

Make sure you're not one of those!

Property can be one of the least tax-efficient ways of passing money on to your children, so if you're investing for their future, it's really important you speak to legal and inheritance tax specialists. You must also make sure that if you own any property jointly with one or more other people you're clear on whether you own it as 'joint tenants' or 'tenants in common'. The first means that if you die, your share passes to the other partner; the second means you can leave your share to who you like in your Will.

Lots of people are a bit slack about making and then updating their Wills, but when you're talking about investing a lot of capital in what are likely to be highly profitable assets, you've got to make sure all your wealth creation efforts don't go to waste if something happens to you.

And before you go signing over ownership of any property assets to your nearest and dearest, check whether that's the right thing to do – it's rarely as straightforward as you might believe it to be.

Get some help from:

- The government website, gov.uk/inheritance-tax/passing-on-home
- Your professional advisors. It's helpful if they can communicate directly with each other to make sure they're all working toward satisfying your wishes

....

"Nobody wants to read about the honest lawyer down the street who does real estate loans and Wills. You have to write about the guys who steal all the money and take off. That's the fun stuff."

John Grisham

Tip 98

Do some joint ventures

Embarking on a property venture with one or more partners can be an exciting and rewarding thing. I have a number of business partners and associates, all of whom I've learned from, while we've each seen great returns on our invested capital.

If you're a bit short of capital but know of a great deal, bringing partners on board can benefit all of you. And it's not always about splitting the capital investment. Sometimes it's about partnering with someone who's quite simply stronger where you're weaker. You might be a pure HMO investor with some capital to invest and get together with someone who has loads of experience in development but no spare cash.

As well as learning new skills, there's the old 'two heads are better than one', and you might find that when you get together with someone on a project, you both become more creative and adventurous, bouncing suggestions and ideas off each other. And, of course, you're doubling your resources, so things often get accomplished more quickly.

This is why networking is so important. Get out and about in your area and meet other investors, entrepreneurs and businesspeople who are all looking to make money and are open to new ideas and interesting ventures.

Get some help from:
- Landlord and local business networking events.
- Good local letting and estate agents. They might know of other landlord investors who are looking to partner with someone.

....

Joint venture, *n.*
A contractual business undertaking between two or more parties. It is similar to a business partnership, with one key difference: partnership usually involves an ongoing, long-term business relationship, whereas a joint venture is based on a single business transaction.

Tip 99

Be very wary about investing overseas

The mad buzz about investing overseas thankfully seems to have disappeared since the heady pre-credit crunch days, when every investor seemed to have a finger in a foreign pie.

The general truth about overseas investing is that you only see huge capital gains if you've got in at the earliest stage of a market's 'emergence', when risk is high and mortgages are virtually impossible to get. Where property was cheap, it was cheap for a reason: there was either massive oversupply or nobody actually wanted to live there.

Developers were throwing up new builds in areas where locals couldn't afford to buy, promising investors that they'd double their money in three years, without actually explaining who was going to buy all these identical apartments when everyone wanted to sell at the same time.

In short, the 'opportunities' sounded exotic and were cheap – some companies would even offer to arrange the financing. Often there were convoluted 'buy back' or 'refinance all your original capital back out' schemes. I haven't heard of a single one that actually worked.

The long and short of it is that it's hard enough to research and make good investments in the market that's on your doorstep, with a currency, language and purchase process you're familiar with, and a legal system you can understand. When all of that's unfamiliar and thousands of miles from home, you really are taking a massive gamble. As far as I'm concerned, it's no longer investing, it's pretty much a lottery.

There are exceptions, of course, but you'd better be ready to ask a lot of questions!

Get some help from:

- Chapter 7 of my book, **'Property Investment Success'**, which goes into a lot more detail about overseas investments and companies that promote them

....

"Sometimes questions are more important than answers."

Nancy Willard

Tip 100

Take care of yourself

Your mind and body will be much more effective - and last longer! - if you take care of them. So take a holistic approach to success and realise that if you keep your own engine room firing on all cylinders, you're more likely to get things done well in other areas of your life, not least your property business. Eat well, exercise and get a good night's sleep. That's it.

....

"Take care of your body. It's the only place you have to live."

Jim Rohn

Tip 101

Keep learning

I've been involved in property virtually all my life and I still learn new things all the time.

One of the things successful people have in common is they tend to like to read. I read at least one book a week to help keep my mind and business on track – and they're by no means all related to property. I enjoy biographies of high-profile people who've reached the top of their game, whatever the field. I think I've read all the property/real estate books that you'll find referenced on courses and in seminars and I always like to check out personal development books that are recommended to me.

Some of these books are exceptionally good, some are pretty bad, but there's always something to be taken from even the bad ones. So keep an open mind and expose yourself to as much material as you can that's inspirational and/or educational.

In terms of the property business, there are so many different opportunities out there and people with great experience and skills that could complement yours, you'd be silly not to take advantage of them. Go to networking events, seminars, business breakfasts, new development launches locally…keep pushing yourself and exposing yourself to bigger and better things.

There's a saying that you should try to surround yourself with people that are more successful than you; I'm not sure that's as important as making sure the people around you are passionate, full of ideas and good at getting things done. Chances are, those types of people will also be successful, but it's positive energy that will keep pushing you forward.

The most important thing to remember is that no matter how good you are at something, there is always more to learn. Don't ever make the mistake of thinking you know it all – you never will!

....

"Anyone who stops learning is old, whether at twenty or eighty. Anyone who keeps learning stays young."
Henry Ford

Even more...

...from Nick Fox Property Mentoring.

Thank you for taking the time to read our book; we hope you've found it helpful. If you'd like to extend your knowledge, please check out our website, where you'll find a wealth of free information and details of our mentoring packages.

We offer a range of mentoring options to suit all needs, from short intensive taster sessions to more comprehensive packages that will give you a deeper understanding of property investment and the buy to let market, focusing on the rewards and implications of building an HMO portfolio.

Various choices available include:
- Half-day 'HMO Education and Tour'
- One-day 'Intensive HMO Property Mentoring Course'
- Two-day 'Intensive HMO Property Mentoring Course'
- 12 months' full access to and support from Nick Fox and his Power Team

Whichever package you choose, you can be assured that Nick's commitment to your personal property goals are absolute. Nick and his team get a real kick out of watching others grow their property portfolios by helping them implement the most successful methods that have been tried and tested over many years.

As skilled and experienced professionals, we present our mentoring sessions in such a way that they are easy to understand, while enabling highly effective learning. The acute insights and practical methodology on offer will help you to take your property business to the next level and secure financial independence for you and your loved ones.

Check out our website **www.nickfox.co.uk** or call us on **01908 930369** to find out more.

Find us on **FACEBOOK** Nick Fox Mentor **TWITTER** @foxytowers
www.nickfox.co.uk **EMAIL** hello@nickfox.co.uk **TEL** 01908 930369
NICK FOX PROPERTY MENTORING
14 Wharfside Bletchley Milton Keynes MK2 2AZ

nickfox
property mentoring

Read on...

Collect the set of books by Nick Fox to help you achieve financial freedom through property investment.

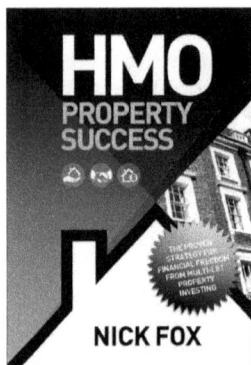

HMO PROPERTY SUCCESS

Do you want a secure financial future that starts sooner, rather than later as you're approaching retirement? By investing in multi-let properties, you can double or even triple the level of rental income generated by single letting, and realise positive cash flow from the start. In this book, multiple business owner and investor, Nick Fox, clearly guides you through the steps to building an HMO portfolio that delivers both on-going income and a tangible pension or lifestyle pot.

ISBN: 978-0-9576516-0-9
RRP: £9.99

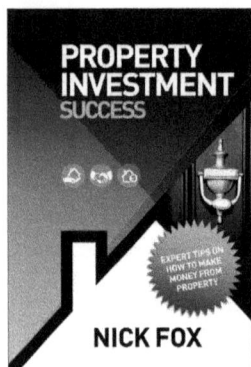

PROPERTY INVESTMENT SUCCESS

How does your financial future look?
If you haven't reviewed your pension provision for a while or aren't completely happy with how your current investments are performing, you should take a closer look at property. In this book, Nick Fox discusses the pros and cons of traditional pensions and makes the case for property as a robust alternative investment vehicle.
He looks at how property can deliver different kinds of returns at different times and shows how you can build a tailored portfolio that perfectly satisfies your own future financial needs.

ISBN: 978-0-9576516-4-7
RRP: £9.99

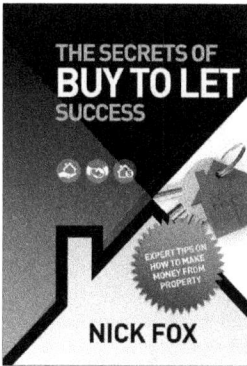

THE SECRETS OF BUY TO LET SUCCESS

Are you looking for a sound investment that can give you both income and growth on your capital, but nervous about the future of the property market? This book will put your mind at rest. In The Secrets of Buy to Let Success, Nick Fox shares his knowledge and expertise about the market, guiding the reader step by step through the basics of building a solid and profitable property business - even through an economic crisis. If you're completely new to property investment, this book is a great place to start.

ISBN: 978-0-9927817-2-9
RRP: £9.99

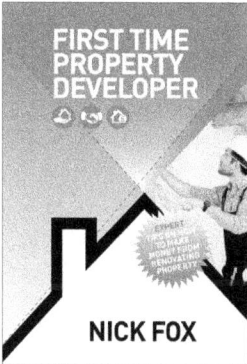

FIRST TIME PROPERTY DEVELOPER

Interested in developing property for profit ? Don't know where to start? Let experienced property expert, Nick Fox, lead you through the process. Nick will show you how to find the property, add genuine value to it by developing and refurbishing and then explain how to sell on for profit or rent out for income.

ISBN: 978-0-9576516-4-7
RRP: £9.99

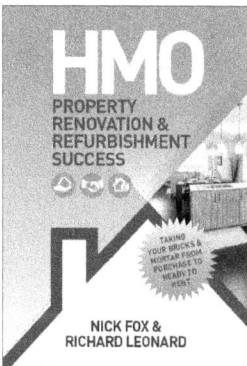

PROPERTY RENNOVATION & REFURBISHMENT SUCCESS

Successful renovation and refurbishment relies on spending the right amount of money in the right way, so are you ready to hone your budgeting, planning and project-management skills? Alongside the deposit, this is where the biggest chunk of your investment funds will be spent. You need to analyse the figures, budget correctly, plan the work in detail and ensure it's carried out properly so that your buy to let performs as you need it to. Not sure how to do that? Then this is the book for you!

ISBN: 978-0-9927817-6-7
RRP: £11.99

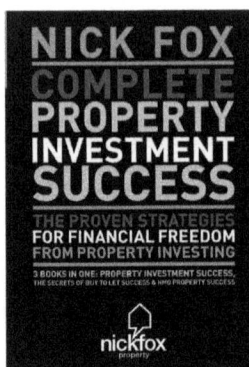

COMPLETE PROPERTY INVESTMENT SUCCESS

This indispensable trilogy takes you through the pros and cons of property as an investment vehicle, looks at the business of buy to let and the different ways you can make money from property, then goes into detail about how to successfully source, refurbish and let out highly cash-positive houses in multiple occupation.

ISBN: 978-0-9927817-0-5
RRP: £26.99

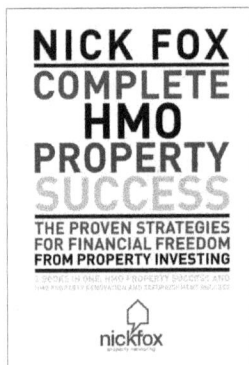

COMPLETE HMO PROPERTY SUCCESS

This HMO 'superbook' is essential reading for anyone who's starting out in property investment and wants to generate income.

It begins by looking at investing in Houses in Multiple Occupation as a business and takes you through how to successfully source, refurbish, let out and manage a highly cash-positive portfolio.

The second part then focuses on the all-important renovation stage. It details how to budget, plan your works, manage your project and carry out the refurbishment in such a way that your HMO performs as you need it to and you get the returns you're looking for.

A prolific and highly successful investor, Nick's personal portfolio extends to more than 200 properties, both shared accommodation and single household lets – and he also has interests in several development projects around the UK.

ISBN: 978-0-9935074-0-3 | RRP: £19.99

Available now online at
www.amazon.co.uk & www.nickfox.co.uk
Books, iBook, Kindle & Audio

Find us on FACEBOOK Nick Fox Mentor TWITTER NickFoxPropertyMentoring
www.nickfox.co.uk EMAIL hello@nickfox.co.uk TEL 01908 930369
NICK FOX PROPERTY MENTORING
14 Wharfside Bletchley Milton Keynes MK2 2AZ

Testimonials

This is just some of the positive feedback I've received from happy mentoring clients over the past few years:

"I met Nick a number of years ago and was immediately struck by his deep knowledge and experience in the field of property investing. No problem is ever too great a challenge for Nick - his creative entrepreneur spirit is a joy to behold. He is both dynamic and detailed, great fun to work with and quite truly inspirational. He is now my business partner and good friend."
Richard Leonard

"Nick and his team are the real deal. Their knowledge and help in moving my investment project forward has been invaluable. Without their expertise I would not have been able to reach my personal property goals or milestones."
Richard Felton, UK

"Great book, great guy and great results for me after I read 'HMO Property Success'. I've now replaced my job with passive income from HMO properties. Thanks, Nick!"
C.Clark, Bedford

"Nick is a very experienced property professional. His practical advice on setting goals, the pros and cons of this type of investment

and how to minimise risks and properly manage a growing portfolio are essential in what can be a very complex investment. Nick's mentoring is not a get-rich-quick formula but a clear and concise way of demonstrating how a solid property investment strategy can be put into action. And the results are well worth it."

D.Wright, Aberdeen

"I have spent money in the past on various property courses, where you are taught in a group in a classroom, and those have not really helped me. This one-to-one mentoring with Nick was brilliant, as I was actually seeing his business and properties, meeting tenants, getting lots of advice and seeing what worked well and what didn't in a live situation. I have booked another two days with Nick in my home city next week, to look at various properties and hopefully start my journey as a full-time property investor, and I cannot wait! I highly recommend this type of mentoring!"

James Robinson, Hull

"Both Sarah and I cannot express how much help Nick has been to our property business over the last two years. His support and knowledge have been invaluable. We would thoroughly recommend his mentoring to any budding investor."

Stuart Lewis, Northampton

"Thank you so much for your patience, professionalism and general understanding during our three-day mentoring programme. The visit to see how your office and HMO business runs was incredible and so, so helpful. Without it we would have been at a complete loss. With your guidance and help we

have now purchased our first HMO property and look forward to keeping in touch to show you our profitable progress!"
Rebecca Santay-Jones, Harrow

"I first met Nick in the autumn of 2012 when I was looking for someone to guide me through my first HMO purchase. Nick's mentoring was invaluable and gave me such a good grounding - not just in HMOs, but in how to run a successful property business - that I have been able to move forward with real confidence as my business has grown. Even now, if there is something I am uncertain of, or I just want to bounce an idea around, I'm very grateful to have Nick in my corner. He has such wide-ranging experience in the industry and I value his opinion greatly. The income my portfolio already provides gives me the option of going part-time in my day job and in the coming months, as I grow the business further, I fully intend to become a full-time property investor and landlord."
Andy Potter, Fareham

"Today's experience has been brilliant – it really opened up my eyes up to the world of HMOs and made me see properties in a different light, in terms of understanding just how much potential each one has. Your experience has accelerated my learning and shown me how important it is to have the right mindset when getting into this area of property investing.

As a kinaesthetic learner, I really enjoyed the hands-on experience of going from property to property and getting a flavour of how you see and do things. Your openness and honesty is what I appreciated the most and has reaffirmed to me that I have made

the right choice. Looking forward to getting that first property!"
Gabriel F, Enfield

"Nick has clearly got a huge amount of knowledge in his field, and having his support and experience has given me the increased confidence to make my first steps into investing."
Craig Smith, Edinburgh